PSYCHODYNAMICS
OF **FEAR, HATE** AND
SOCIAL POLARIZATION

ANTONIO R. BARQUET

authorHOUSE®

AuthorHouse™
1663 Liberty Drive
Bloomington, IN 47403
www.authorhouse.com
Phone: 1 (800) 839-8640

Published by AuthorHouse: 11/02/2018

ISBN: 978-1-5462-6669-3 (sc)
ISBN: 978-1-5462-6668-6 (hc)
ISBN: 978-1-5462-6667-9 (e)

Library of Congress Control Number: 2018913181

Print information available on the last page.

Any people depicted in stock imagery provided by Unsplash.

This book is printed on acid-free paper.

CONTENTS

DEDICATION

THIS BOOK IS dedicated to the late Dr. Alberto Iglesias—physician, mentor, colleague, friend, teacher, and spiritual father. He was a physician of physicians and doctor of doctors whose knowledge of psychiatry was surpassed only by his compassion for orders. As a beacon of light for many suffering from the storms of the mind, his passing is a great loss for humanity.

DEDICATION

The world in which we live is a product of our thinking. In order to change it, we must change the way we think.

—Albert Einstein

My people are destroyed for lack of knowledge; because you have rejected knowledge, I reject you from being a priest to me.

—Hosea 4:6

PREFACE

IT IS WITH some sadness that I begin to write this book—sadness because I am beginning to see a polarization dividing society that is getting worse as time goes by and is beginning to divide us in deeper and deeper ways. If this polarization is not brought under control and its mechanism understood, we will reach a point where our own survival as a species will be at stake. The mechanism of this polarization on a superficial level appears to be based on different sets of values, interests, and philosophies. At a deeper level all this polarization has a common denominator that is not recognized and is contributing to the fragmentation of our society. As we will see in the rest of this book this polarization has a psychological basis. We teach our youngsters in school about science, mathematics, philosophy, arts, driver's education, and sports; however, we do not teach them the most important aspect of their education, which is how to know themselves and understand the motivation behind their actions. The purpose of this book is to try to fill that void in the educational system and provide a source of knowledge for individuals who wish to understand themselves better.

We need to have a paradigm shift in the way we think about ourselves and the world around us. The only way we can accomplish this is by understanding deeply the mechanisms that motivate us and how they interact with one another. This understanding comes at a heavy price. Gaining any insight into the mechanisms of one's self is by nature a painful process in which the self itself feels threatened and scared. It takes courage to see our own selves and their mechanisms and to accept with humility some of the conclusions at which we arrive. Unless we are willing to pay this price personally and individually now, we will pay it later at a higher price as society.

I respectfully ask for the reader forgiveness. In my prior book, *Why Are You? A Sense of Identity*, I was remiss in not explaining fully some of the concepts that explained human behavior. I wrongly assumed that the concepts explained were self-evident and needed few explanations. After taking questions from many readers I became aware that clarification of some of these concepts was necessary. In this book I try to explain those concepts more fully so that the associations between them and human behavior are more clear. I am a man of few words (I find words superfluous) so this will be a difficult task for me, and I respectfully ask for the reader's patience and tolerance. This book is not pleasant to read. It is not designed to pamper, entertain, or indulge the ego (I leave that to entertainment authors). It is a profound examination of our behavior and, as such, it requires intellectual muscle and courage to be able to understand it and go through it. It may cause psychological pain. Read at your own peril.

> Human beings tend to learn two ways—either by example or by concussion. Concussion hurts. The choice is ours.
>
> —Unknown

CHAPTER 1

The Driving Force

Don't curse the darkness; light a candle.

—Unknown

Curiosity will conquer fear even more than bravery will.

—James Stephen

THE SENSE OF self develops as a mechanism of the evolution of the species. This might go against the religious belief systems of many traditions; however, as we shall see farther down, it doesn't contradict the presence of a divinity but actually may enhance it. Let us understand this concept.

We take the sense of self to be a unique attribute of the human species, but, actually, several species are beginning to exhibit a primitive sense of self or identity. For example, some dolphins are able to recognize themselves in a mirror and actually try to remove some paint that has been placed on their cheeks when they see it in the mirror. Likewise, some chimpanzees and great apes appear to have a primitive sense of self. I remember a story told to me by a friend from South America, who used to like hunting. In his younger years he went hunting in a forest and shot a monkey. He remembers the monkey touching the gunshot wound, looking at its hand, and then beginning to scream when it realized it had been hurt. This suggests the presence or recognition of a self—albeit at a very primitive level. So we cannot assume to have the predominant or preeminent presence of a unique self.

So how does the presence of a self facilitate the mechanism of evolution in a species? At a very basic and simple level, the sense of self helps to preserve the organism by allowing it to determine whether another organism is small enough to eat or large enough to be eaten by. For example, it is said that alligators will attack only prey that is about one third their size, suggesting a very primitive and basic sense of self. This allows for a delineation of body boundaries, which allows the organism to either hunt or escape being hunted. But at a more advanced level, the main attribute of having a self is the ability to have the mechanism of identification, and for this, you need a sense of identity. (You can only have a sense of advanced identity if you have the concept of self-existence.) This mechanism (identification), which appears to be automatic and subconscious, facilitates the introjection of values and behavior patterns that may be advantageous toward the species.

Let me give an example. Suppose there is a primitive society living at the edge of the ocean. Their main source of nutrition might be fish. Let us suppose that there are a number of fishermen in the society and that one of them has the habit of getting up at five o'clock in the morning, starting a little bonfire, dancing around the fire, and praying to a palm tree he believes to be a deity. He goes out fishing and comes back with a large load of fish. The rest of the fishermen get up around ten o'clock in the morning, go straight out to fish, and come back with only a handful of fish. After looking at this, the general population may start imitating the behavior and values of the first fisherman.

The fact that he is a successful fisherman has nothing to do with the fire, dancing, or praying to the palm tree; it's that he gets up at five o'clock in the morning when the fish are apparently actively feeding, migrating, or crossing. This story demonstrates the mechanism of identification at work, in which society tends to adopt or incorporate into their behavior patterns or thought processes that they believe facilitate the process of survival. This mechanism of identification has an advantage over genetic adaptability in that genetic adaptability takes generations to develop, whereas the identification process facilitates a mechanism of adaptability in a nonspecialized organism in terms of weeks or months as opposed to generations. In a rapidly changing environment, this becomes an evolutionary advantage.

From a more realistic and modern viewpoint, we can observe the identification process when an individual goes to the movies, for example. If the movie is an action movie, individuals will tend to identify with the hero of the movie. They will tend to introject and begin mimicking the behavior pattern and perhaps some of the values of the hero. Likewise, when adolescents begin to follow a singer, they tend to dress and act like and even adopt some mannerisms from this new idol. In this manner, they are beginning to introject a behavior pattern and even a set of values into their personalities. This gives them a sense of identity, which is based on the acquisition of affective fuels of ego integration, which we will discuss later.

Contrary to what many people think, evolution is a two-way street. When you have a macroenvironment and there are microorganisms (not *microorganisms* in the sense of bacteria or similar microorganisms, but *microorganisms* in that they are small relative to the macroenvironment) in that environment, evolution tends to take place at the level of the microorganisms, with the environment remaining relatively stable. However, if the organism grows to a significant size, it begins to affect the macroenvironment. This change in the macroenvironment then triggers another evolutionary change in the microorganism. The net result is that evolution becomes a two-way street where the macroenvironment changes in response to a large population load of microorganisms, and in turn the microorganisms must again adapt in response to the macroenvironmental change induced by its population.

A clear example of this taking place is global warming. For many centuries when the human population was a small, global warming was not a significant factor and was mostly dependent on environmental changes (volcanoes, eruptions, storms, etc.). In the latter centuries as the human population has grown significantly, it is beginning to induce global warming on a macro scale, which in turn is forcing many other living organisms to adapt—with the loss of some species and possibly the dawn of many new species, which are adapting to the new climate temperature. Our ability to think about and observe these changes is probably what gives us a chance to prevent them from taking place and to save many species that otherwise would be lost secondary to our actions. On the other side it is precisely the fact that we have a sense of self that tends to be concerned with its own survival that works against this realization and prevents us from taking action.

So what is the problem with having a sense of self if it is a mechanism of evolution for the survival of the species? The main problem is that when the organism develops awareness of its own self-existence, a profound fear of nonexistence automatically appears. In other words, if I exist, then the possibility is present that I may cease to exist. This fear goes hand in hand with existence. You cannot have one without the other. It is the price we pay for having a sense of self or existence. And here precisely lies the problem, because that fear is the driving force behind most of the actions of the self.

So how can we see the fear and the effect it has on the sense of the self? We can begin to see this fear in two ways. Everyone at one point or another in life has experienced a sense of humiliation, either by another individual or by a set of circumstances. So let me ask: Why does one feel uncomfortable when one is humiliated? If you ask a lot of people, you would get different answers. Most will say they feel that they are less confident when they are humiliated. Others may say they fear that people may think less of them, and still others may say that they failed to live up to their expectations. The most common answer, however, will be that they feel that they are less. Let us call this a technical term: *ego contraction*. Likewise, let's call the sensation that they failed to live up to their expectations a *lack of ego expansion*. The next question is why an ego contraction is unpleasant. To begin to comprehend this fear, we will need to extrapolate the concept of ego contraction.

In mathematics there is the concept of a limit of a function. For example, when talking about a derivative, the definition is the limit of a function when delta X tends toward 0. We can use this concept and ask ourselves about the limit of an infinite number of ego contractions. In other words, if one contraction is followed by another and then another one, what is the endpoint? It becomes obvious that the endpoint will be what I call the *zero point*—nothingness or nonexistence. This is the reason that humiliation feels uncomfortable. The sense of self feels threatened by an ego contraction because it is looking at the end point of nothingness or nonexistence as a possible reality.

Let's try a different strategy. Let us look now at fears. What is the biggest fear a person may have? Fear of losing your life, fear of losing your job, fear of losing a loved one, or fear of sickness? Let us take fear of losing a job. Why is one afraid of losing a job? A person may say that if one loses a job, one may not be able to pay the bills and eventually lose the house; the spouse may file for a divorce. Furthermore, one may be left homeless, sick, and exposed to the elements, without access to health care. The endpoint is that now that this individual may die, and death implies nonexistence or nothingness. By promising an afterlife, religion becomes a coping mechanism for guaranteeing the sense of self-existence after death. Observe that the endpoint of this fear is again the possibility of nonexistence, the zero point, or nothingness. You can make the same analysis for any fear a person may have. If you follow it all the way to the end you will find you reach the same conclusion or end point.

So we can understand that an ego contraction makes individuals feels threatened precisely because the end point of it is a sense of nothingness or nonexistence. Let us go back to the prior paragraph and examine briefly a lack of ego expansion. A lack of ego expansion may also threaten the sense of self because it doesn't provide the self with a mechanism to feel safer or more secure against this fear. It so happens that ego expansion is the mechanism whereby the self integrates or solidifies itself against this fear. This ego expansion is predicated upon the acquisition of what I call affective fuels of ego integration.

So why do I use this term *affective fuels of ego integration*, what are these fuels, and how can they be identified? The word *fuels* refers to the fact that this is a mechanism of ego solidification that is continuously being used and expended. It has to be continuously replenished like gasoline in a car. *Affective* means that it has to do with affection. As we shall see, affection probably integrates the sense of self on the basis of emotions through a neurobiochemical process (I leave this research to the neurobiologists). *Ego integration* refers to the fact that these fuels solidify or strengthen the sense of self against this primary fear of nonexistence.

How can we identify the affective fuels of ego integration, and where do we look for them? It would be smart to look for them in the places where people deal with the sense of self and the negation of the self—the monasteries of the different religious traditions. They all have several common characteristics. First, monasteries tend to be isolated or set apart from society. Here we identify the first fuel, social fuel. Social isolation is very destructive, especially when it is not voluntary but it is imposed by circumstances. Second, individuals are given a religious adviser so that they don't feel superior or special for holding a specific belief system. This is the second fuel, religious fuel. Third, individuals usually live in poverty or take vows of poverty, a demonstration of material fuel, the third fuel. Fourth, individuals also take vows of humility—the fourth fuel, intellectual fuel—as well as vows of celibacy, the fifth fuel, emotional–sexual fuel.

In the different religious traditions, some or all of these fuels are present to some degree or another. The integration process of the ego begins at the level of the protoego probably between the third and fourth years of life, and likely even earlier. The different stages in the child, as described by various psychology schools, are essentially the child's attempts to begin to integrate the sense of self by controlling or achieving dominance over a particular fuel of ego integration as a mechanism of developing identity. If we look closely at the different stages, we will observe that, beginning with control of one's bodily functions, the organism is essentially trying to establish acquisition or possession of a particular fuel of ego integration. As a child develops, that control extends to other fuels, culminating in the intellectual fuel as a main mechanism of self-identity in most of the population, with some exceptions.

Individuals will tend to solidify their sense of identity by integrating themselves in the easiest and most efficient fuel available, depending on the circumstances. We will see in a later chapter how this tends to radicalize some individuals with religious fuel.

During the integrative process, the social and religious fuels are usually the ones acquired earlier and will serve as filters for other fuels acquired later in life. Once established, they will allow or block other fuels from integrating the sense of self. In essence, they become the equivalent of Freud's superego, or conscience. These fuels are usually acquired from the parents, immediate family, and surrounding social structures in the young individual, as well as slightly later by the religious education that individuals receive.

Almost simultaneously, if individuals are in an industrial and modern society, they begin to develop intellectual fuel in the form of elementary, high school, and college education. The acquisition of intellectual fuel eventually leads to their being able to maintain a job or a means of subsistence, buying a house (material fuel), and forming a family. The formation of a family is the acquisition of emotional-sexual fuel to complete this cycle of identity in the individual. Observe that the fuels are acquired in a somewhat specific order, although some overlapping in the acquisition of the fuels tends to take place during the development of the sense of identity. This overlapping does not negate the fact that these fuels tend to peak at different stages of development in a generally specific order.

It should be pointed out that within each set of the five fuels, there are subsets and possibly even sub-subsets. At times these subsets may conflict with one another. These conflicts will be explored further when we discuss the social fuel as a mechanism of polarization.

All of these fuels compose the sense of identity of an individual. They all answer the question, "Who am I?"

- I am in as much as society respects me or appreciates me. (Social fuel)
- I am in as much as God loves me. (Religious fuel)
- I am in as much as I have achieved. (Intellectual fuel)
- I am in as much as I have. (Material fuel)
- I am in as much as I am loved. (Emotional-sexual fuel)

Our sense of identity is predicated on these five fuels of ego integration, and the polarization that we see in our society is based on them.

CHAPTER 2

The Etiology of Psychological Pain

There is no coming to consciousness without pain. People will do anything, no matter how absurd, in order to avoid facing their own soul. One does not become enlightened by imagining figures of light, but by making the darkness conscious.

—Carl G. Jung

No man is free who is not master of himself.

—Epictetus

No man is master of himself who doesn't know himself.

—A. Barquet

ONCE WE UNDERSTAND that the self is threatened by the end point of nonexistence and that it defends or integrates itself against this nonexistence by utilizing affective fuels, we can then understand the mechanism of psychological pain. Psychological pain has three roots:

1. the loss of or expected loss of affective fuel of ego integration; leads to an ego contraction
2. the lack of acquisition or the expected lack of acquisition of an affective fuel of ego integration; leads to a lack of ego expansion
3. fragmentation of union; leads to a sense of incompleteness

Observe that I talked not only about a loss or lack of acquisition but also about an expected loss or expected lack of acquisition. One is as important as the other.

Let us examine the first concept, the loss or expected loss of an affective fuel of ego integration. What do we understand to be a loss? If individuals are integrated on a material fuel—for example, a house—and they lose the house, the sense of self will suffer an ego contraction, which will make the individuals feel threatened by nonexistence. This will cause discomfort or psychological pain. Likewise, if individuals lose their careers or a loved one, the same process will take place and the individuals will feel threatened by the end point of nonexistence, or zero point. The manner in which the affected fuel is lost will, to a point, determine the reaction of the individual. For example, if the individuals lose a house to a fire or a natural disaster, they may feel depressed or despondent but not aggressive. If, on the other hand, they decide to join a monastery, the house may feel like a burden, and getting rid of it may actually feel like a liberating experience. However, if the house is taken away from them by a government or by another person acting unjustly, they may feel aggressive and react with violence to the loss of the affective fuel. Observe that in all three circumstances, the house is lost, but the reaction is different. In two of the circumstances, there is a loss of material fuel with a subsequent ego contraction that in one case generates depression and in the other causes aggression, depending how the house is lost. If the house is lost to natural causes, the individuals accept the loss of affective fuel with a subsequent ego contraction since they don't feel directly threatened by the event, although they get depressed. If the house is taken away from them unfairly, though, the subsequent ego contraction is now more powerful because they feel that the ego contraction or threat was directed at them specifically. Then the individuals respond with violence (depending on the social and religious filters). In the other case, if the individuals want to join a monastery, the house becomes a burden and it is actually a liberating experience to get rid of it. The reason this feels like a liberating experience is because the individuals are expecting to substitute the social affective fuel and religious fuel of the monastery for the material fuel of the house. Since there is a substitution of one affective fuel for another, the sense of self doesn't feel threatened and actually looks forward to letting go of the house with the expectation of receiving the other affective fuels in the monastery. (The determination of which affective fuel the sense of self wishes to integrate depends in large part on the social and religious fuels learned during the development of the protoego. Remember that the social and religious fuels serve as filters for the other fuels that come later in life.)

Let us examine now the expected loss of an affective fuel. Let's go back to the house. If individuals cannot pay the mortgage on the house and the bank proceeds with foreclose, they will expect the loss of an affective fuel (material fuel) and will feel anxiety for that reason. Again, the threat of the loss of an affective fuel triggers an expected ego contraction and makes the sense of self feel threatened by nonexistence. Observe that both the actual loss and the threat of a loss of an affective fuel of ego integration lead to psychological pain.

Let us examine now how the lack of acquisition or expected lack of acquisition of an affective fuel causes psychological pain. Take the example of students who wish to go to medical school. If they are looking forward to gaining admission to medical school, this is because they are expecting a mechanism of ego integration based on intellectual fuel that will provide them in the future with more fuels in the form of material and emotional-sexual fuel. It may also be that they were taught that they would be more respected (social fuel) or that those expectations were placed on them by the family and social circles. If the individuals fail to be admitted to medical school, they will possibly suffer an ego contraction from the intellectual point of view but also a lack of ego expansion in the long term. The immediate psychological pain resulting from the frustration of not being accepted leads to an ego contraction, but the lack of an ego expansion in the future also leads to anxiety because the self will feel threatened by the inability to obtain an affective fuel of ego integration that they thought would give them more security in the future. At this point we need to understand that the fear of nonexistence is ever present throughout the lifetime of an individual. After every integrative process, the sense of self feels temporary relief from this fear, but after a while the fear reappears. It is for this reason that the lack of acquisition of an affective fuel of ego integration causes anxiety because the self perceives it would not be able to defend itself from this fear in the future due to not having that expected affective fuel.

By the same logic, the expected loss of an affective fuel integration will cause anxiety. If the students described above apply to medical school but feel that they may be turned down or not accepted, they may anticipate the loss of an affective fuel with the subsequent fear of lack of integration in the future, and this will cause psychological anxiety

Observe that in both circumstances A and B, it is the fear of nonexistence that is the driving force behind the anxiety and psychological pain the individuals experience. One must be able to clearly see and understand this fear to be able to appreciate the mechanism by which it causes psychological pain. One can try to explain psychological pain as lack of self-esteem, lack of love, loss of self-respect, fear, sickness, and so on, but if you follow every single one of these explanations to its end point, you will find that at the very bottom of each and every single one of them, the fear of nonexistence is the driving force behind the pain.

To understand how the loss of union causes pain, one must understand that it has two different effects as the mechanism. If a person is married, the loss of the spouse or a loved one implies a loss of affective fuel of the social and emotional-sexual types, and of course ego contraction. This ego contraction will cause the sense of self to feel more threatened by nonexistence and therefore will cause psychological pain. This is the first level. On a deeper level, one needs to understand the concept of union from the religious point of view. In the Christian, Buddhist, and Hindu traditions, there is the concept of union with the universe or with one another. The concept of original sin, which will be described later as a religious affective fuel, can be considered to be a separation from that "absolute" if we assume the existence of a god, so we can understand the concept of original sin as the acquisition of self-consciousness. This consciousness allows us to determine good and evil in terms related to the sense of self and thus the name "the tree of knowledge" as the tree from which Adam and Eve cannot eat is described in Genesis in the Bible. If we assume that there is a universal consciousness and that the taking of self-consciousness separates us from it, then the concept of a loss of union begins to make more sense. So the loss of union causes pain at the deeper level because the individual, once he is separated from this absolute but has acquired consciousness, tries to re-create that union in the imperfect things around him. For example, the individual may look for this imperfect union in friends, in attachment to a particular soccer or football team, in professional societies, in family members, in nationalism, and so on. You get the idea. In other words, we look for this sense of union that we lost through the taking of consciousness in imperfect things around us. The separation from this universal consciousness causes psychological pain by making the sense of self feel incomplete, isolated, and fractionated. On a more human level, the loss of a loved one, whether it is a child, spouse, or a dear friend, re-creates this separation and causes the sense of self to feel fractured or incomplete again. This in turn makes it feel more threatened by nonexistence. Individuals feel the imperfect separation from a human being and then re-create the "perfect" separation from the absolute, with the taking of consciousness. The end result is a profound sense of pain, not so much from the loss or lack of acquisition of an affective fuel but from the separation from that union with another individual, which makes their sense of self feel fractionated and threatened. From this perspective, the eating of an apple as described in the Bible represents the sense of self beginning to consume affective fuels (in this case, the apple represents material fuel). You need a sense of self in order to feel the need for affective fuels. Hence, the analogy of Adam eating an apple.

In Buddhism, the root of suffering is attachment. Buddhists consider that attachments are what cause pain and suffering. They understand intuitively the mechanism of psychological pain, but they fail to see the fear of nonexistence as the driving force. These attachments that they refer to are the affective fuels of ego integration. Losing one of the affective fuels leads to an ego contraction, and therefore psychological pain as described above as the sense of self feels more threatened by nonexistence—hence, the concept that attachments cause pain and suffering.

Emotions and Affective Fuels

Understanding now that the concept of pain and suffering derives from the threat of nonexistence and from the three mechanisms of loss, lack of acquisition, and fragmentation of union, we can also understand how these would cause a sense of sadness, grieving, despair, and other emotions associated with negative stimuli. The opposite is also true. If individuals are able to acquire affective fuels and their sense of self feels an expansion and makes the ego feels safer against nonexistence, they will feel a positive emotion, such as happiness, excitement, peace, and even gratitude. So emotions can be related whether they are positive or negative to the gain or loss of affective fuels. According to Robert Plutchik's (a brilliant individual) theory, there are eight basic emotions. Let's analyze them from the new perspective of affective fuels.

> **Fear**: From the perspective of affective fuels, fear encompasses the expected loss of an affective fuel with the subsequent expected contraction of the sense of self that is feeling threatened by nonexistence.
>
> **Anger:** Anger occurs when individuals feel that an affective fuel that they are entitled to is taken away or that an ego contraction is induced by another individual or circumstances. The threshold for anger depends on several factors, which include how much of an integration the individuals have on a particular affective fuel and the circumstances in which this affective fuel is taken away from them.
>
> **Sadness**: Sadness is mostly related to the fragmentation of union. It can also be associated with the loss of an affective fuel. The circumstances, however, are usually ones in which individuals realize that the loss or fragmentation of union that they experience is outside their control and is not brought on directly against them. For example, a person dying from a natural disease would induce a feeling of sadness in the partner.

However, if the person were to be killed by a drunk driver in an accident, then the partner would also have concomitant feelings of anger toward the driver.

Joy: Joy can be understood as the acquisition of an affective fuel either spontaneously, like a gift, or as a reward for one's work. For example, students who graduate after going to college for four years experience a sense of joy in acquiring a diploma. The diploma represents social recognition of the effort that they put into obtaining a certain degree of knowledge, which they in turn believe will make them able to obtain other affective fuels and give a sense of safety from nonexistence.

Disgust: This emotion can be triggered when individuals' own affective fuels are not recognized or appreciated by another. This challenges their ego stability and makes them question the affective fuels that they have for integration. For example, if an individual has a daughter and expects her to clean her room in the morning after waking up but she does not perform that expected behavior, the individual may feel the sensation of disgust. Likewise, individuals who expect society to behave in a certain way toward them may feel disgust when this behavior is not performed. Also, an individual may see a beggar being mistreated by a group of young truants. The individual may feel disgusted because the social affective fuel that he himself has and that he extrapolates to other people is being threatened by the behavior of the truants, which contradict this social fuel. The sensation of disgust usually does not rise to the level of anger because it does not involve the direct loss of an affective fuel. The sensation of disgust usually involves the concept that one's affective fuels are not being shared by somebody else, and this raises a level of threat to the stability of the self. The individual recognizes that he himself may not be under direct threat, but the fact that the other person has different affective fuels shakes the beliefs in the ones he has.

Surprise: Surprise can be positive or negative, but usually it is taken in the positive sense. It entails the sudden acquisition of an affective fuel of integration or a sense of union that was not expected or anticipated.

Trust: Trust derives from the expectation that another individual will deliver an affective fuel or is reliable to continue to deliver an affective fuel.

Anticipation: Anticipation is essentially the expectation of receiving an affective fuel, which will help the self feel more protected against nonexistence. It can also be a negative emotion in anticipation of something that will decrease the affective fuel and make the self feel threatened.

As we can see, emotions are closely related to the acquisition or loss of affective fuels in the desire to stabilize the sense of self against nonexistence or induce a contraction of the sense of self, which would make people feel more threatened.

It should be mentioned that there appears to be a hierarchy and an economic aspect to the process of integration by affective fuels. As previously mentioned, the first affective fuel that is integrated is a social fuel because of the immediacy of the family and environment. Social fuel will then give way to religious fuel as a second mechanism of integration if the family holds religious values. The parents, brothers, uncles and aunts, and grandparents all contribute to the social fuel, and they begin instituting in children the hopes, fears, prejudices, and aspirations based on their own mechanisms of integration. This first fuel then becomes the first filter through which later fuels will be integrated. The religious fuel, once integrated, may actually overcome the social fuel as a filter of integration. This happens because the religious fuel is the one that most directly answers the fear of nonexistence. If individuals integrated themselves to a large extent with this fuel, it may actually substitute the social fuel as a filter of integration. For example, it may label certain other fuels to be acquired later as sinful and may threaten the individuals with permanent punishment if they accept these other fuels. As we can see, that appears to be a hierarchy in the order in which these fuels are acquired. The economics of fuel integration depend on how easy and effective the acquisition of fuel integration becomes. If individuals have access to many fuels of integration—for example, education, social interaction, material fuel, cars, houses, and so on—the tendency is to integrate on multiple fuels at the same time. If, on the other hand, people live in a deprived environment and the only fuel available is the religious fuel (which is free and easily accessible), the tendency would be to integrate a sense of self on this particular fuel. One can see that the economics of the fuel depends on how accessible it is and how effectively it integrates the sense of self. This integration by fuels other than the religious and social fuels is highly modulated by the filters established by the social and religious fuels, respectively, which occur in an earlier stage of development.

In makes sense, then, that in order to evaluate a patient, we must try to determine first which affective fuels act like filters for the other fuels that the individual would use for ego integration.

The social and religious fuels will determine not only which other fuels will come into the sense of self to integrate it but also how the integration process itself will be accomplished. For example, suppose that a woman has a father who is a professional. She may be coaxed by the father to become a professional herself. The father may give her affection when she accomplishes intellectual feats, thereby programming her to expect attention (affection) when she does well in school. He is in essence teaching his daughter to become integrated by intellectual achievements. If she is able to attain a career and become a successful professional, then she will feel integrated and will solidify her sense of self. If, on the other hand, down the line, she fails to become a professional and is not able to achieve the professional goals that she thought would give her a sense of integration, she will become frustrated and develop psychological pain.

However, another individual may have parents who emphasize physical ability because they like sports. The mother and the father may be basketball fans or baseball fans. The individual may feel that she gets affection from her parents when she is playing sports or doing well in sports. She may carry this mechanism of integration into adulthood by becoming a sports player herself or excelling at a particular sport. If she doesn't play sports, she may drift into coaching a baseball team or a basketball team. Her mechanism of ego integration is based on sports.

Observe that in both circumstances, the individuals' sense of identity will be predicated on the type of accomplishments that provided her with affection from the parents during the early years and that she carried into adulthood.

Religious fuel will also serve to determine how the sense of self integrates itself. If parents are very religious, they instill in their children a strong sense of moral commitment, and the children find that they receive attention and affection when they go to church or do good deeds, then the children may feel inclined to become priests or ministers because, in that way, they can feel that they receive affection and love from God. Religious fuel also establishes the moral compass of individuals by establishing a conscience and a concept of right and wrong.

Observe that the initial mechanisms of ego integration will depend on receiving affection from the parents in a very basic way, and as the person grows into adulthood, then the mechanism of receiving attention (affection) advances to more mature forms.

The mechanism of ego integration by receiving affection from the parents may be substituted by another mechanism if individuals feel that they cannot obtain affection from the parents by meeting their expectations. For example, a boy may have two parents who are professionals and who give attention to the child when he excels at school or achieves some intellectual goals. The child, however, may have difficulty in school but be very good at sports. He may notice that he gets affection not from the parents because of his grades, but he gets attention from his coach and his fellow students at school when he excels at sports. The child may start substituting the affection and attention from his coach and his fellow students for exceling at sports for that he wants from his parents since the affection and attention he receives from his fellow students serve to integrate a sense of self and develop his identity.

Cases may develop in which individuals are very smart and their parents expect them to do well in school, but the environment is not conducive for intellectual development—for example, individuals who are far removed from society or live in a tribal area. Even if these individuals desire to develop themselves intellectually, they may be limited in that endeavor by their circumstances. In that case, they may choose to integrate themselves in a different manner more consistent with the environment. The sense of self is in itself pliable, and the mechanism of integration is also flexible and affected by the environment.

As we can see, the mechanism of inguinal integration will depend not only on the preconditions for the parents' affections but also on individuals' abilities and alternative forms of receiving affection, the environment, and the facilities to develop a specific fuel of integration. We can start seeing now hierarchy and the economics of ego integration work, depending on several factors. The sense of self will do whatever it takes to achieve integration, whether by standard, established ways or by hook and crook.

When dealing with a patient or individual with emotional problems, based on personality development (not biochemical disorders such as schizophrenia or overt psychosis), the therapist may be faced with one of three options to help the individual. Understanding that affective fuels tend to integrate the ego, therapy should be directed toward these affective fuels. The three options are (1) reinforcement, (2) substitution, and (3) introspection. Let us discuss each one in detail.

The mechanism of reinforcement essentially reinforces or stabilizes the affective fuel that is failing in an individual. For example, if individuals are integrated in the intellectual fuel and suffer a demotion or a loss of status of the intellectual fuel, they may suffer depression. By reinforcing other achievements intellectually that they may have accomplished over time, they can stabilize this affective fuel and reinforce its integrative mechanism of the self. For example, they can emphasize the fact that they have earned a degree, are respected in the community, have been able to make a living, and so on. Many times this so-called failure of findings integrative fuel is secondary to expectations placed on individuals by society and by the professional milieu in which they works.

The second mechanism, substitution, should be employed when the failure of the main integrative fuel is of such a degree that it cannot be reinforced—for example, an individual who lost a spouse with a concomitant loss of emotional-sexual fuel cannot be reinforced. In this instance, substitution by explaining to the individual that he or she can rely on friends, nearby family, and children may help the individual integrate his or her sense of self and maintain emotional stability.

The third mechanism, introspection, should be reserved for individuals who desire to understand their behavior more deeply and who have the intelligence or education to be able to understand the concept of affective fuels and how this mechanism integrates the sense of identity. The first two mechanisms are relatively easy to apply and require relatively little time in order to stabilize the sense of self. The third mechanism takes longer and requires more prolonged psychotherapy in order for individuals to understand its effects on their behavior. Depending on the clinical condition of the patient, one may have to choose which mechanism to apply. For example, an individual who is severely depressed due to the recent loss of a loved one is in no position to try to understand this mechanism since the sense of self is in an extreme state of pain due to the threat of nonexistence. In this case, it would be inappropriate to try to help the patient through introspection. An appropriate approach would be to substitute or reinforce the other affective fuels in order to stabilize the individual and alleviate the psychological pain. Once this stabilization takes place, then one may proceed to the mechanism of introspection if the patient is able to understand or desires to go this route.

The affective psychological pain due to the loss of affective fuel should not be taken lightly. We are witnessing now in society a marked increase in adolescent suicide due to different pressures that society is putting on them. Suicide can be subdivided into active suicide and passive suicide. Active suicide occurs when the patient suffers an acute loss of affective fuel, the sense of self suffers an acute contraction that makes it more vulnerable to the fear of nonexistence, and individuals prefer to take their own lives rather than live with the pain of that contraction. There is a profound lack of understanding regarding where the psychological pain comes from in these individuals. All they can feel is the pain, not the mechanism of the pain. At this point, since the event is acute, reinforcement and substitution are the main processes to try to save suicidal individuals and stabilize the sense of self. Once they are stable and the danger of suicide has passed, then we can try to explain to the individual the mechanism of introspection.

Pertaining specifically to adolescents, the trigger mechanisms for suicide can be seen in the acute loss of affective fuels. The proliferation of social media makes the rejection of an individual widespread rather than limited to a small, specific group of people. The widespread rejection threatens the social fuel on which the adolescents rely to a large degree. During the adolescent years, individuals will try to shift the affective fuels from the family to the social circle in which they operate in order to become independent of the affective fuel of the family. Adolescents begin to perceive the potential loss of affective fuel from the family, along with the realization that they are dependent on that affective fuel and that the loss of a parent or a family can terminate that fuel. In an attempt to achieve security, they will try to shift the social fuel from the parents to the social circle in which they operate in order to achieve control and feel independent of the social fuel of the family. If the attempt to transfer this fuel from the family to the social circle fails, the sense of self will suffer an acute contraction, and in the absence of other integrative mechanisms, this contraction can be significant and lead to profound pain, leading to suicide. This is compounded by the fact that at that age, individuals still lack other integrative mechanisms. For example, due to the lack of education, they don't have an intellectual fuel to integrate, which leads also to a lack of material fuel and a lack of emotional-sexual fuel since they cannot yet obtain a family (spouse). This contraction can be aggravated further if the individuals have a girlfriend or boyfriend and get rejected by that person. It should be mentioned that the contraction is aggravated by the fact that adolescents integrate primarily on one affective fuel; the sense of self is not integrated on a variety of them, which would dampen or ameliorate the sense of contraction. If the individuals are integrated on the emotional-sexual fuel—for example, a girlfriend—and suffer a rejection, in the absence of other integrative fuels this can also lead to suicide. To understand this better, consider that adolescents have a dependency on the family. The family provides all five affective fuels of ego integration: social affective fuel; religious fuel by teaching the adolescent about moral values; material fuel in the form of housing, food, and clothing; intellectual fuel by providing an education; and emotional-sexual fuel by the affection of the mother and father. Adolescents realize the potential danger of losing the family and all the affective fuels. This dependency, then, leads them to attempt to establish affective fuels outside the family so that they can exert control over them. This transition phase can fail, which then leads to a profound identity crisis in adolescents. This is the reason many parents perceive a rebellion in their adolescents, which is nothing more than an attempt to establish affective fuels outside the parental influence and establish a sense of identity. In the absence of other integrative mechanisms, the failure of adolescents to integrate themselves on a particular chosen one can lead to disastrous consequences to the sense of self and eventually suicide.

Another form of suicide is passive suicide. The difference between passive suicide and active suicide is that in active suicide, a profound failure of one of the main integrative mechanisms leads to profound pain and the decision to take one's life. In the absence of dampening mechanisms such as the use of social fuel that makes suicide a sin or a socially unacceptable behavior, individuals will take their own lives. This is modulated by religion and society. In Japanese society, *seppuku* or *hara-kiri* is an acceptable way of ending one's life in order to preserve honor. In this aspect, societal values modify suicide. On the other hand, in the Christian religion, taking one's life constitutes a sin, and this prevents many people from attempting it. Again, we see the religion modifying suicide.

Passive suicide takes place when individuals are prevented from committing active suicide by religious or societal values, or the loss of integrative fuels of ego integration is progressive and not acute. In this case, individuals may opt to stop taking care of themselves, leading to a progressive deterioration in their physical being. They may gain weight, become obese, and develop hypertension. They may start drinking alcohol and mixing it with sleeping pills. The end result is a decline of their physical health, or even an "accidental" overdose. In reality, they have lost the will to live due to the loss of affective fuels, and rather than killing themselves actively, they prefer to do it in a passive way by ceasing to take care of themselves. This is usually preceded by depression or despondency that is not perceived by family or friends.

A very common occurrence is suicide among first responders. Suicide can result when people are subjected to a lot of stress for a long period of time—in other words, posttraumatic stress disorder (PTSD). The mechanism of suicide in first responders with PTSD can be triggered by two events: (1) the intensity of the trauma and (2) the repetitive nature or constancy of the trauma.

How does trauma cause PTSD in an individual? In order to understand, we have to understand the mechanism whereby this stress is caused. Once people are exposed to a very intense trauma and see themselves or other people injured in a severe way, they reach a profound realization of the danger to their own existence. This realization comes directly if the individuals are the ones who are injured and therefore realize their own mortality (i.e., potential for nonexistence) or indirectly from seeing others injured because they identify with them and think, *That could have been me.* Both mechanisms make the individuals realize the danger of nonexistence and threaten the sense of self significantly. The second mechanism, the constancy or repetitiveness of the stressful event, does not allow the sense of self to obtain compensatory mechanisms through the acquisition of affective fuels, which normally serve to stabilize the sense of self against the fear of nonexistence. So, for example, individuals in the middle of a war may be subjected to social, religious, material, intellectual, and emotional deprivations due to the circumstances, preventing the sense of self from reinforcing their integration mechanisms and inducing a sustained ego contraction, which makes the sense of self more threatened by nonexistence. This sense of threat against the sense of self is what is understood as "anxiety." Some individuals, depending on how the sense of self is structured in terms of the affective fuels, may be able to overcome PTSD if they have mechanisms that allow for the sense of self to restructure itself utilizing a specific affective fuel. If the individuals' main affective fuel of ego integration is the one that is threatened, they are more prone to suffer from PTSD than individuals whose secondary affective fuel of ego integration is threatened while the main affective fuel of integration is left untouched. For example, some individuals may have their sense of integration based in their own self-reliance, in which case an outside threat will serve only to reinforce this self-reliance. On the other hand, if their main source of integration is a social fuel and they lose it, they may feel more threatened in their mechanism of the ego integration. Since each individual has different mechanisms of ego integration, the susceptibility to PTSD will vary from individual to individual. Children are more susceptible to traumatic events precisely because their mechanisms of ego integration are not yet fully developed and they depend more on the parents to obtain the affective fuels of ego integration. It is for this reason that the loss of a parent is severely traumatic for a child. The sense of self may use several coping mechanisms to protect itself. For example, psychologists recognize regression, in which the individual tries to protect the sense of self by going back to an earlier stage where integration of the sense of self is based on more simple and easily acquired affective fuels. Psychologists also recognize repetition compulsion, in which the trauma is relived over and over again after it has been repressed and may be triggered by events in which the sense of self already integrated after the event. In this case, the sense of self suffers a threat to one of the integrative mechanisms that it used to stabilize itself after the event. When this affective fuel is threatened, the traumatic event memories may reappear. By trying to cope with the traumatic event, the sense of self may also be trying to reaffirm its existence by proving that it can survive it again. Alternatively, it may be trying new strategies of ego integration until it finds one that it can utilize to integrate itself and feel safe in the face of the event. Because of the ignorance of the integrative mechanisms, many times individuals are unable to process the trauma and work through it. The repetitive compulsion becomes an ineffective way of trying to deal with trauma.

The fact that many psychologists believe that preexisting somatization and anxiety disorders exist in these patients (in other words, prior difficulty or ineffective ego integration with affective fuels) reinforces the concept that some individuals may be more susceptible to PTSD due to the inability to effectively integrate the sense of self with affective fuels. Dissociation is another mechanism recognized by psychologists in which individuals dissociate or see themselves apart from the situation taking place. This is initially understood as the sense of self trying to protect its integrity by dividing the self into an experiencing self and an observing self. (Psychologists believe that this dissociation can lead to the feeling of depersonalization, in which the individuals feel like they're merely onlookers and not experiencing the traumatic event, or it may lead to derealization, in which individuals feel they experienced the traumatic event as a dream.) The main drive of this mechanism is to protect the sense of self from nonexistence. Dissociation makes the mechanisms of coping with the trauma less effective because the ego stops trying to integrate itself with affective fuels and opts to essentially protect its concept of self by separating the pain from the concept of self that remains. Since the integrative mechanism is not present, this mechanism is ineffective in protecting the sense of self and allowing it to feel secure so that it can overcome the trauma and the threat to its existence. The price that is paid is that individuals are exposed to experiencing the pain over and over again since it has not been able to overcome the fear of it through mechanisms of integration to reaffirm its existence.

Therapy in these individuals should be directed by the three concepts explained earlier—reinforcement, substitution, and introspection. The patient should be examined to determine which mechanisms of ego integration he or she possesses, and then the therapist should try to reinforce the ones that he or she has and substitute the ones that cannot be reinforced. And if the individual has the capacity, then introspection should be attempted so that he or she can understand the mechanism.

CHAPTER 3

Mechanism of Prejudice and Other Behaviors from the Perspective of the Concept of Affective Fuels

Prejudice is the child of ignorance
Love of enlightenment

—Unknown

If you can't explain it simply, you don't understand it well enough.

—Albert Einstein

Prejudice

TO UNDERSTAND THE mechanism of prejudice, we need to understand first the reason we have a sense of self. As previously explained, the sense of self serves as an evolutionary mechanism that allows for the organism's quick adaptation to the environment by introjecting a behavior pattern through the mechanism of identification. The main advantage of having a sense of self and the mechanism of identification secondary to it is that the adaptation process takes place in a matter of days, weeks, or months rather than genetically through several generations. One obviously sees the temporal advantage of having an adaptive process take place over a short period of time rather than a longer period of time. This is especially advantageous if the environment is changing at a fast rate, and the genetics cannot keep up with it due to the timing involved in achieving a genetic shift in order for adaptation.

Understanding this, we can now begin to see how it plays a role in the mechanism of prejudice. Faced with the fear of nonexistence, which we have described before and which is primal in every sentient being, individuals integrate themselves in an affective fuel in order to solidify the sense of existence. If a group of people is associated with a lower class, individuals who feel the prejudice are taught that acquiring or mimicking the behavior pattern of that group will make them "less." Out of fear of becoming less, individuals will block the identification process and reject people from that group because they feel that becoming like them will cause them to be threatened by nonexistence. This is, in essence, the profound mechanism of prejudice.

Some modifications of this mechanism may take place, but the basic mechanism is the one we have described above. For example, this may begin when two tribal groups are exposed to each other. In this situation, the individuals from one tribal group may have a sense of identity already formed. When the first group is exposed to the other tribal group with different patterns of behaviors, the first tribal group feels threatened in its own sense of identity. The reaction of the first tribal group would be to reject the other tribal group, even though the behavior pattern of the second tribal group may be more advantageous for survival than that of the first tribal group. The reason for this is again a profound fear of nonexistence, against which the sense of self has been integrated from a very early age on affective fuels to protect itself from that fear. The exposure to different behavior patterns presents a threat to the identity of the first tribal group, and rejection occurs. Again, note that the main mechanism or driving force is that primal fear of nonexistence. An example of this situation can be seen in modern-day Europe, which is experiencing the influx of many groups from different communities that have been torn apart by the ravages of war and civil strife. The immigrant groups already have been integrated from a very early age or specific social, and religious affective fuels. Instead of adapting and interjecting the new values and behaviors from the host society, they reject them and try to maintain the same behavior patterns that led to their failed societies in the first place. This lack of integration is prevented precisely because of the fear of nonexistence and the fear of letting go of prior affective fuels of ego integration.

Another side effect of prejudice is the mechanism of feeling superior to other people through rejecting them. This sensation of superiority corresponds to an ego expansion, which in essence makes the sense of self feel more secure against the fear of nonexistence.

Thus the mechanism of prejudice in essence prevents an ego contraction by the mechanism of identification by rejecting the individuals but also leads to an ego expansion by the sensation of feeling superior, which protects the sense of self from nonexistence.

Mechanism of Forgiveness

Forgiveness takes place at different levels. At the first level, one forgives because one feels better by doing so. The mechanism for this is that the individuals' religious affective fuels tell them that it is good to forgive because it is what is expected. In other words, the individuals reinforce the religious affective fuel and feel better within themselves by the act of forgiveness. This is the most basic level of forgiveness.

The second level of forgiveness involves liberation. When people wrong someone, they usually do that by taking away an affective fuel of ego integration from the second person. The second individual who has been hurt by this action may desire revenge based on the social affective fuel, and it may or may not be obtained. If it is obtained, it does not replace the affective fuel that was taken away by the first person. There is a transient sense of ego expansion; however, the fear of nonexistence reappears and the sense of emptiness returns. So a sense of emptiness still prevails. If it is not obtained, it causes psychological pain due to the lack of acquisition of an affective fuel. When people forgive, they liberate themselves from the need to acquire an affective fuel, and the sense of self feels free to pursue other fuels, which decreases the anxiety.

The third level of forgiveness is deeper and involves the people who have been hurt realizing the ignorance of those who have hurt them. This ignorance pertains to the lack of understanding of the need for affective fuels and its mechanism by the individual who hurt the other person. One religious leader acknowledges this mechanism. When

Christ is dying on the cross, he calls out to his father and implores him to forgive those who crucify him because "they do not know what they're doing." Here he recognizes the ignorance of humankind with regard to the motivating factors of their behavior.

At an even deeper level yet, we forgive because we recognize our own ignorance in the other person. This then begins to touch on the concept of unity and the realization of the oneness with the other person. From the historical point of view, Christ realized this also when he instituted the Eucharist (the concept of "communion" or common-union, found in many Christian sects). So, although he did not explicitly say so during his crucifixion, that message of unity was already there. This same concept of unity appears in Buddhism, with the caveat that if there is no self, then there is no self to be wronged and forgiveness is not necessary.

Likewise, a more radical way of thinking about this is the concept of "loving your enemy," which was also espoused and put forward by Christ. This seems to be counterintuitive at first glimpse. However, if we subject it to a careful analysis, it may actually make sense. Why would you love one who wants to hurt you?

From a personal point of view, loving your enemy denies the self the social affective fuel of revenge. As explained before, this is also a form of liberation from the need for acquisition as explained in a prior chapter. It also helps to humanize the other individual, facilitating the concept of union. But what is the effect on the other individual? The other person has been taught to hate because he or she has been taught that you are trying to take away one of his or her affective fuels of ego integration and thus decreasing his or her sense of self. The moment you show this person love, his or her perception of you, in terms of trying to take away an affective fuel of ego integration, begins to change. Instead of seeing you as a mechanism of ego destruction, he or she begins to see you as a mechanism of ego integration. It becomes harder for this person to dehumanize you, and he or she begins to allow the humanization process through identification to begin. This in turn facilitates the development of a bond of unity. In addition, returning love for hate challenges his or her moral code, which is also based on learned affective social and religious fuels, making it necessary for him or her to transform it. So what seems to be counterintuitive from the beginning actually begins to make a lot of sense.

Anatomy of a Kiss

Why do we kiss people? If you think about it carefully, why do we kiss people we care about instead of, for example, pulling their ears or tugging their noses? The reason that we kiss is that, when we eat, we bring something to the mouth. We essentially incorporate that which we are eating into our selves by consuming it. When we kiss someone, we are subconsciously desiring to incorporate that person into our selves. By the act of kissing, we are bringing someone to our mouths and sucking that person in the act of kissing. We are essentially trying to be one with the person, and we are trying to satisfy the desire for union that I spoke of in a prior chapter.

Mechanism of Ambition

The mechanism of ambition is based on the fear of losing an affective fuel. The sense of self integrates itself on the material fuel. The fear of losing that material fuel leads the sense of self to try to acquire more material fuel to feel more secure. Once an expansion of the self has taken place through the acquisition of material fuel, a temporary sense of well-being results because of the new ego expansion. After a while, the fear of nonexistence reappears, and the self begins to look for new material fuel to expand a second time in an attempt to feel secure again. After each expansion, the fear reappears, making this a vicious cycle. This is why there is no end to ambition or greed; after every expansion, the fear of nonexistence reappears. Observe that although both components— fear of loss and lack of acquisition—may be present, it is the fear of loss that is the driving force behind ambition.

Mechanism of Jealousy

The mechanism of jealousy is based on the lack of acquisition of an affective fuel. Individuals base their sense of self or ego expansion on the prospective acquisition of attention (emotional-sexual fuel) from another person. They look forward to an ego expansion through this acquisition and the sensation of feeling that they are more or exist more with that attention. When they lack that attention or sense that attention is directed toward another person, they feel that they are less because of the lack of acquisition. This is the mechanism of jealousy.

Mechanism of Envy

The mechanism of envy is also based on the concept of lack of acquisition, except this time it is directed toward the acquisition of a material affective fuel rather than the acquisition of an emotional-sexual fuel. People have the concept that they would be more or exist more if they had more of what another person has. It is similar to the mechanism of ambition, with the difference that in the mechanism of ambition it is the fear of loss that is driving the ego, whereas in the mechanism of envy it is the lack of acquisition. Observe that in all these mechanisms (except for the mechanisms of forgiveness and of love, which we will discuss shortly), the fear of nonexistence and the need to integrate the sense of self against that fear by utilizing different affective fuels are the driving mechanisms.

Mechanism of Love

In order to understand the mechanism of love, we need to make a separation between infatuation and true love. Infatuation has to do more with the concept of expected acquisition of emotional-sexual fuel as a mechanism of ego integration, whereas true love actually denies the self and is more closely related to the concept of unity. (I will discuss the concept of unity again in the religious section, which I think is more appropriate.) For now, let me give a brief definition of *love:* "True love is the profound realization of your true nature in the other individual." This definition was given to me by the Reverend Joshu Sasaki Roshi, a Zen master, and it has taken me almost a lifetime to understand its meaning. It has its basis, not in the mechanism of infatuation, but in the mechanism of unity and the profound realization of the oneness that we have with one another. I shall discuss this further under the heading of religious affective fuel.

Mechanism of a Phobia

The mechanism of a phobia in terms of affective fuels can be understood again from the basis of the fear of nonexistence. Anxiety is an ill-defined fear that has no solid base, precisely because it is very difficult to define *nonexistence*. People may have a profound fear of nonexistence itself or may have a fear of loss of an affective fuel at a secondary level—that is, a specific fear, such as the loss of parental affection, loss of status, or loss of material things. Understand that the secondary fears, if tracked backward, will eventually end up in nonexistence. People may find it easier to handle this loss by transferring fears to a specific object or circumstance that allows them to control the fear by avoiding the specific object or circumstance. By objectifying the fear, they are able to escape the constant presence of this more profound fear and continue living their lives.

Mechanism of Bullying

Physical and social bullying are commonplace, and the latter has become more so with the advent of technology. Those who do the bullying do so because they feel a sensation of power and control when they do. Why do bullies desire power and control? It should be obvious that it causes an ego expansion to make them feel safer against the fear of nonexistence. By putting others down, they feels superior, and by feeling superior, they feel that their existence is ensured against this primal fear of nonexistence. Unfortunately, bullying is typically aimed younger people, among whom these mechanisms and this primal fear are not evident, so the mechanism of bullying will continue. There are several forms of bullying, and they are all based on the five affective fuels. Social bullying, for example, involves individuals who humiliate or make others feel inferior because they don't belong to a specific class. Religious bullying is very common in the Middle East, primarily targeting people in religious minorities. Intellectual bullying is another type in which, for example, individuals make others feel inferior because they go to a more prominent university or educational institution. Material bullying involves wealthier people making others feel inferior by the use of material fuel (examples abound), and finally, you have emotional–sexual bullying, which is very common in the rejection of homosexuals and in high school when people gang up against a particular boy or girl and expose their sexual behavior. Although these types of bullying have the common element of our primary fear of nonexistence, the sad part is the lack of introspection by many of the individuals doing the bullying.

Mechanism of Hate

Hate develops when individuals begin to associate another person or group with the expected loss or lack of acquisition of an affective fuel. For example, some people may feel that a specific group of people desire to take away what they consider to be one of their rights. We can take as an example a union worker who feels that her medical insurance plan may be terminated. If she feels that she depends heavily on this medical plan due to circumstances beyond her control and that the people who want to terminate the plan belongs to the corporate class, then she will develop animosity and hatred toward these people. The intensity of the hatred would be modulated by how important and numerous the affective fuels are as a mechanism of integration for the worker. For example, individuals who base their sense of integration on their race and solely on race may feel more threatened by a group of people who are calling for racial equality. They therefore may feel hatred toward this group of people. By the same token, an individual who desires to acquire racial equality and feels that the other is diminishing him may feel also threatened by the other individual and will react with hatred also towards the individual who makes him feel less. This becomes then a two way street. Martin Luther King, a moral giant was able to transcend this hatred by the mechanism of forgiveness

Mechanism of Adolescent Rebellion

In order to understand the mechanism of adolescent rebellion, or misbehavior, one has to understand several factors. First, during the early formative years, the family provides the child with all the affective fuels of integration. They provide a house and food (material fuel). They provide religion and social interaction (social fuel). They provide an education, and they provide emotional affective fuels in the form of affection and parental love. At about puberty or adolescence, individuals begin to realize their dependence on this affective fuel from the parents. Subconsciously, they may begin to fear the loss of affective fuel with the realization that parents are not eternal, and at some point they will disappear. At this point, the adolescents may wish to transfer the acquisition of affective fuels from the parents and the family, which they do not control, to affective fuels on the outside, which they can control. So they try to make this switch in order to feel secure that the affective fuels that they are obtaining do not depend on another person but rather on themselves. This is a form of "self-realization" in the sense that the individual controls the affective fuels that they need for their integration. Once their education is complete and the children are able to make a living on their own, buy a house, and have a family, they usually returns to the parental fold but now from a different perspective. As adults, they cherish the love and affection of their parents because they have been able to break free from the dependence on the parental affective fuels. In essence, during the rebellion, adolescents are trying to establish control of affective fuels of integration to break this dependence on the parents and reassure their sense of self that they now control those affective fuels. They may look for acceptance from peers (social fuel), decide to obtain a summer job (material fuel), have a girlfriend or boyfriend (emotional-sexual fuel), and even decide to move out or into the basement of the house to have privacy. From the religious point of view, they may decide to follow the religion that was taught to them or to look for a different religious belief system that helps integrate their sense of self.

It is at this a stage that social media becomes extremely dangerous. Before it existed, individuals were exposed to only a handful of friends or companions, but now with social media, they may have thousands of "friends." Their social fuel may be based on the acceptance of thousands of anonymous friends. Since adolescents are very vulnerable to rejection at this point because they are in a transition phase trying to look for affective fuels outside of parental influence, a major rejection by way of social media can lead to a profound ego contraction and even suicide. It is important that the parents become involved with adolescents to reinforce and help them make the transition so they can obtain these affective fuels and see the relativity of the likes and dislikes that abound on social media but do not truly represent the mechanism of integration for them. They have to teach adolescents to stand on their own two feet and have personal opinions of themselves, rather than base their sense of self and value on the likes of dislikes of others.

Depression

Depression has several causes, including biochemical, genetic, and environmental. Several studies have shown that depression can be treated with medications as well as with psychoanalysis. From the environmental point of view, when individuals lose acutely one of the affective fuels of ego integration—for example, the loss of a loved one or a job—they may feel an acute ego contraction and develop what is called a situational depression. Most of the time, individuals will recover from this depression once they are able to integrate their sense of self on a different affective fuel, reinforce their prior affective fuel, or substitute their prior affective fuel. It may happen, however, that the individuals see no hope in the possibility of acquiring a different affective fuel ego integration. When this happens, individuals may go into an apathy phase and lose interest in the reintegration of the self. At this point, the depression may become chronic, and medical as well as psychological intervention is needed. The brain is known to have plasticity; in other words, it is able to accommodate and change some of the biochemical processes in response to environmental situations. If the loss of an affective fuel is strong enough, it can trigger such a change and make depression long-lasting. Therapy should be directed toward reinforcing or substituting a prior affective fuel or individuals may go into a refractory phase of an ego contraction. They may feel that there is no escape from this ego contraction or from the fear of nonexistence and that attempts to find a new affective fuel of integration will not be successful in making them feel that they are worth something (ego expansion). This may occur when people don't have the ability to look for a new fuel of ego integration, to replace the old fuel of ego integration, or to obtain a new fuel of ego integration. For example, if in old age a man loses his partner, his chances of finding another individual to provide him with affection are decreased. The inability to go back on the dating scene may maintain his depression by making it difficult for him to replace the affective fuel of ego integration that he found in his partner. Eventually, if the man is able, then engaging in introspection can be attempted so that he understands the mechanism.

Motivation

Motivation is closely related to depression; it is its opposite mechanism. Motivation is the desire of the sense of self to obtain an affective fuel of ego integration that individuals believe can lead to an ego expansion and make them feel better in the face of the fear of nonexistence. Many motivational speakers essentially go into mechanisms of substitution of one affective fuel for another. For example, if people are overweight due to overheating (material fuel or self-compensation), a motivational speaker may try to point out that if they lose weight, they would be accepted and admired by members of the opposite sex and obtain emotional-sexual affective fuel. The substitution will work, provided that filters of social and religious fuel place this second substitution above the original compensatory affective fuel. Observe that the motivation of the speaker is essentially substituting one affective fuel for another. If the individuals value eating more than admiration or, in this case, emotional-sexual fuel, they would not be able to make the transition and substitute one fuel for another. The ability to make the substitution depends on the original filters of social and religious fuel and in what priority order the individuals place the affective fuels. If they place the necessity of emotional-sexual fuel above the material fuel (food), then they will be able to make the transition. If, on the other hand, they place more emphasis on the material fuel than on the emotional-sexual fuel, then the transition will not take place. Usually, emotional-sexual fuel is more directly correlated with affection and therefore will tend to outweigh the material, intellectual, social, and possibly religious fuels. It should be pointed out that emotional-sexual fuel overlaps with social fuel in the sense that a partner satisfies most of the social and emotional-sexual components of the affective fuel for ego integration.

People who are gregarious (social fuel) tend to be so by nature, and therefore this fuel usually overcomes the others. Motivational speakers are highly lacking in depth of knowledge of the mechanisms of ego integration. They are essentially merchants of affective fuels, peddling one affective fuel over the other. They should instead be focusing on the mechanism of integration and allowing for individuals to become free of the mechanism of ego integration.

Motivation for an affective fuel is modulated by the social and religious fuels learned at an early age. For example, if children are taught that money and respect are important and that a way to obtain these is through a professional career, they may work hard to obtain a professional career in order to obtain the other two. The concept of self-realization (nothing wrong with it), in which an individual is able to achieve self-satisfaction by acquiring a profession or an intellectual endeavor, is another way in which the sense of self feels an ego expansion and feels more protected from nonexistence. This should be encouraged because a side effect of intellectual pursuits is very often the opening of the mind to more inquisitive endeavors and hopefully some degree of introspection into the sense of self.

Sadomasochism

To understand the mechanism of masochism, first we need to understand several basic premises.

- Individuals who engage in masochism have a need for affection during the integrative years.
- During the early, formative years, these individuals learn that the mechanism to obtain attention from the dominant figures (sublimated affection) in their lives is to experience pain and submit themselves to this pain so that the dominant figures, who may or may not enjoy causing pain, pay them attention. (Negative attention is still attention. For example, it may be the attention paid to a misbehaving child, who may be misbehaving in order to obtain any sort of attention, even if it is negative.)

- There may or may not be an element of denial of their own biological identity, such as in homosexuality, and pain is a mechanism to psychologically destroy their sense of identity.
- The connection with sexual behavior gives a physical equivalent to the psychological desire for affection from dominant figures by submitting themselves to pain.
- Once the sexual behavior begins, the conditioning reflex takes over and becomes established behavior.
- There may or may not be a mechanism of identification with the dominant figures who are causing the pain depending on the psychological makeup of the individuals.

To understand sadism, we can do a similar analysis.

- Individuals who engage in sadism do so to obtain attention by inflicting pain on someone else. The fear that they causes in other individuals is a form of attention since the submissive individuals are concerned about the pain and direct their attention toward them at all times.
- The fact that they are exerting control over other people serves to make them feel superior, which is the equivalent of an ego expansion, and makes them feel safer against nonexistence.
- There may or may not be an element of identification with the submissive individuals, again depending on the psychological makeup of the sadist people.
- The connection with sexual behavior again gives a physical equivalent to the psychological pleasure that the individuals experience by inflicting pain.
- Once the sexual behavior begins, the conditioning reflex takes over and makes it a repetitive behavior.

I mentioned an element of identification that may or may not be present. Let me explain this. In some fetishes—for example, macrophilia (giantess fetish)—individuals may identify with an object that the giantess is crushing as a way to destroy their sense of identity. Many times, this is secondary to the fact that they are latent homosexuals who reject overt homosexuality due to the filters of social and religious fuels and who also reject their male sense of identity. At the same time that the individuals are identifying with the object being crushed by the giantess, they may also identify with the woman doing the crushing because of their desire to be a woman. The identification would be stronger if the woman experienced pleasure in the act of crushing the object. For a more thorough and complete explanation of fetishes, the reader is referred to chapter 9 of the book *Why Are You? A Sense of Identity*, where I explain this mechanism in full detail and give several in-depth examples of the mechanism of a fetish. This dual-identification process may or may not take place in individuals depending on their specific psychological needs. The other processes, however, are present.

Mechanism of Pedophilia

To understand the mechanism of pedophilia, we must understand several concepts.

- Pedophiles are essentially looking for affection, to integrate the sense of self.
- At some point during their development, they realized that children get attention and affection and learned this as a mechanism to obtain affection. They may have been impressed with the reaction of a child or a very emotive child in response to affection. Such an experience created a lasting impression, and they desired to be that child to obtain that affection. The identification process had begun.
- Through the process of identification, pedophiles identified with the children as they tried to sexually excite them, thus achieving indirect affection through the process of identification with the children.
- There may be a component of power over the children, which also contributes to integrate the sense of self, and the pedophiles may also enjoy the sensation of power because it makes them feel more secure against the fear of nonexistence.

- The sexualization that takes place when they abuse children is a form of "physicalizing" this affection to solidify or intensify the sensation of affection.

One must differentiate true pedophilia, which is based on the mechanism of identification with the child, from pseudo or predatory pedophilia. Predatory pedophilia is not based on the process of identification; rather, these individuals prey on the innocence or vulnerability of children in order to take advantage of and satisfy their own sexual desires, which are heterosexually oriented. An example of this is what happened in the Rotherham scandal in England, where individuals took advantage of many innocent girls in order to satisfy their sexual desires. Although neither of these types can be justified, predatory pedophilia carries a graver concern because it reduces the other human being to an object and denotes profound selfishness and dehumanization, many times finding justification in a religious belief system.

Mechanism of Hoarding

To understand the mechanism of hoarding, we need to understand the concept of affective fuel quantification. Let us try to understand this with an example. Suppose that some individuals are so devoid of affection that they look for affection from animals. They may lack the social, intellectual, material, and religious fuel to integrate their sense of self. They rely only on the emotional fuel of affection from an animal. This answers the question "Who am I?" with "I am inasmuch as the animal loves me." So these individuals rely on the affection of animals to feel compensated for the lack of direct or sublimated affection caused by the lack of other affective fuels. The question goes as follows: if one animal loves me, two animals love me slightly more, and fifty animals love me fifty times as much. In other words, the individuals quantify the affection by quantifying the number of animals that they have. Another component that may be inherent in this is the fear of losing the only source of affection, which is compensated by having more than one source of affection. This leads to the acquisition of more animals to ensure continuity of affection, in case one is lost. The individuals may get to the point where they substitute the social human fuel—that is, human society—with the society of the animals with which they live. This society of animals replaces human interaction and human affection, does not reject the individuals, and is dependent on them, becoming a symbiotic relationship. The individuals obtain an affective fuel that they need to integrate the sense of self, and the animals obtain food and shelter, as well as some degree of affection. For an in-depth example of this behavior, the reader is referred to chapter 9 of the book *Why Are You? A Sense of Identity*.

Mechanism of Homosexuality and Alternative Sexual Behavior

(This section is reproduced from the book *Why Are You? A Sense of Identity* and is included here for completion sake since I thought it would be pertinent.)

Emotional-sexual fuel can explain homosexuality, fetishes, and pedophilia. Presently, there are two main currents of thought about the origin of homosexuality: that it has a genetic component and that it is mostly acquired. I suspect the truth is somewhere in between. The genetic part may result from certain children's increased need for affection, and the acquired part may be due to unsatisfied needs for affection and the ego's attempt to integrate itself and look for this affection. In a prior chapter, I mentioned the importance of parental affection to the well-being and development of children; it integrates the ego when children are between three and four. What happens when father figures fail to give affection to children or are threatening figures to children? Several mechanisms will illustrate how the sense of self tries to integrate itself when faced with this problem. Sex becomes the hook to obtain affection. In the case of male children who are denied affection or are threatened, they will try to obtain affection indirectly. They may think, *My father doesn't like me, but he likes my mother. If I become like my mother, my father will like me.* Their protoegos begin to identify with the mother in an attempt to obtain the father's affection. By identifying with the mother, they develop submissive characteristics, which are less challenging to the father, so that he will not react with hostility toward them. This is akin to an animal's showing submissive behavior to a pack leader. In this way, the children feel less threatened and try to be the object of the father's affection, a coping mechanism. Note the similarity between the biological and psychological submissive behavior to the leader of the pack—in this case, the father (or even more precisely, the dominant figure regardless of the sex).

With girls, the same identification process may take place, but it is directed elsewhere. Recently in our family, a situation developed. One of the paternal family members with two daughters is very much into sports and such activities, and he began pushing his daughters into sports in an intense way. Their sports were mostly male oriented, so the daughters began sensing that their father paid attention to them when they became like boys and therefore acted this way to obtain their father's affection and attention. Through the repetitive identification process, their ego integration learned to assume male characteristics, and they both became gay. Their sense of self became integrated as that of males to gain the affection of the father. Once it is integrated like this, the sense of self has learned this as a coping or survival mechanism to get acceptance and, indirectly, affection.

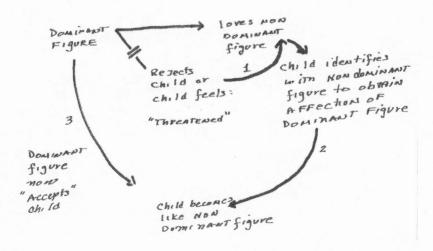

Another process that is more subtle and occurs later in life is the process of identification of an adult with a woman or man, depending on the sex. For example, a promiscuous man may place a mirror in the bedroom to watch himself having sex. If a woman is very expressive, he may start the identification process subconsciously with her. In the process, the sense of self or ego may start reforming itself by identifying more with the female. There comes a point when the process of ego integration is so advanced that the person, through the identification with the woman, begins to react with a man—in this case, himself—in the mirror. After all, the woman is expressing pleasure, and by concentrating on her, he begins to react through her. After a while, he can develop homosexual tendencies. The ego membrane is permeable and capable of expanding and contracting; it is also capable of reforming itself. The sense of self should not be construed as something fixed and rigid, incapable of change, but rather as something fluid and flexible, able to reform itself by introjection, reconstruction, and deletion of certain aspects of the affective fuels that it uses for integration.

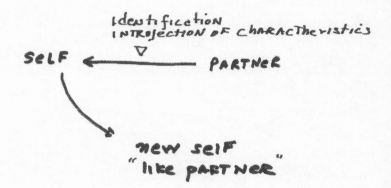

Another condition that may develop is narcissism. This frequently occurs, for example, when a man begins to lift weights and looks at himself in the mirror at the gym. He begins to admire the male figure in his image. Some degree of pleasure is present in having a good body. By reacting to the male figure in the mirror, the individual begins to develop affective reflexes toward other males, a process that may lead to homosexuality in a very subtle way.

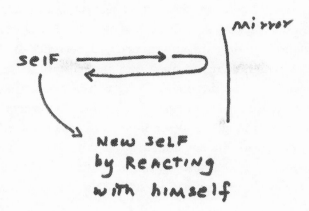

Another mechanism that occurs as a cause of homosexuality is the inadvertent identification with the woman while watching pornographic films. Here, the attention of the man is directed not to what he's feeling but to what the woman is experiencing when she has sex with another man. By concentrating on her, he identifies with the pleasure she exhibits. Through this process, he begins to reform his sense of self, and given enough time, he could develop affective reflexes of the homosexual type. Years ago, while I was researching the subject, I overheard someone who was into pornography tell another that he preferred one porn film over another because the woman was more expressive in the film he preferred. Subconsciously, he was identifying with the woman since it was easier to identify with someone giving expressive manifestations. This process of identification sometimes occurs at a subconscious level, where the person is not aware of any behavior that may be ingrained and done automatically in our psyches as part of a survival mechanism. These are some of the possible mechanisms in which the need for affection at the level of the self and the ability to use the identification process for ego integration may trigger homosexual behavior. It is the dominant figure in a relationship who appears to determine homosexual behavior. In most relationships, this is the father, but it could be the mother if she is the dominant figure. The same thing applies to same-sex couples; one may be the dominant figure, the leader of the pack that defends the group, leads the group to food supplies, mates with the females in the pack, and determines which individuals remain in the herd. The protoego, in an attempt to feel safe and protected, will do whatever it takes to obtain the affection and protection of the dominant figure. So how does the sexual part come into this equation? It is important to understand this aspect. Sex becomes the hook used by the person who is trying to survive to maintain the attention of the dominant figure. If the dominant figure is interested in a submissive individual because he offers him sex, his relative self-survival is assured. At the same time, the submissive individual has to be able to enjoy sex while being passive for this equation to work. Therefore, in the integrity process of the sense of self, if the person feels threatened by a dominant figure, he will become passive to satisfy both sides of the equation—to get the attention of the dominant figure and to enjoy sex from a passive point of view. The same reasoning can be applied but in reverse to the case of female homosexuals.

This need for the self to maintain its integration and to survive is the basis for Stockholm syndrome, in which a hostage who faces a very threatening situation physically and psychologically begins identifying with the hostage taker to preserve life and sense of self. Observe that there is a direct link between the survival of the self and the physical being. In homosexuality, if a father is very abusive or threatening, the child's sense of self will introject the female characteristics of the wife or partner via the process of identification in order to survive. The child is helpless, just like a hostage, and tries to survive a perceived threat by identifying with the woman, whom the child perceives to be an object that receives affection. This passivity is not threatening to the leader of the pack. The reason the child identifies with the mother is that, at this early age, the ego is not well defined yet and is looking for affection. In the case of an adult with Stockholm syndrome, the sense of self is already well defined but pliable, and by identifying with the ideology of the hostage taker, the adult is identifying with a source of affection; the hostage taker is devoted to and loves an ideology that becomes the equivalent of the woman, what appears to be the object of affection to the child (hostage). Thus we see that the same process is active in both Stockholm syndrome and in the child needing affection who becomes homosexual.

When I alluded to the fear of nonexistence at the beginning of this book, it was not a haphazard allusion. The self tries to integrate itself and exist. This is also linked to the survival of the physical organism in a very direct way. In both Stockholm syndrome and homosexuality, the effort is to survive. The sense of self is a beast. Let me repeat this: *the sense of self is a beast.* It will do whatever it takes to integrate itself and survive. You cannot explain this integration process and the force with which it is done unless you understand that it is driven by the fear of nonexistence of the psychic and the physical self. Let us discuss the mechanism by which sexual variations and deviations occur. Of the many psychologists and psychiatrists I have spoken with, few are able to explain to me the difference between a fetish and homosexuality. Let's do it here. I will make a statement that will appear to be controversial but will become obvious as we progress in the explanation. Homosexuality and fetishes are variations of mechanisms to obtain affection; a fetish is disguised homosexuality. First, let us do the comparison and then the explanation. We will consider homosexual characteristics and parallel them with two or three fetishes.

TABLE 1. Femdom Domination

Homosexuality	Female domination or femdom
Dominated by a male	Dominated by a woman (the woman is a male in disguise)
Passive behavior	The woman exhibits dominant behavior.
Rejects his identity or sexuality	The woman humiliates and degrades the man's identity—normally the man is dominant.
Wishes to be a woman	The man identifies with the woman and the pleasure she manifests while she dominates him.

Homosexuality	The man has a macrophilia fetish (giantess).
Dominated by a male	The giant woman dominates the shrunken man.
Passive behavior	The shrunken man is a sexual object of the giantess—passive.
Rejects his identity or sexuality	The man is crushed by the giantess, destroying his identity.
Wishes to be a woman	The man identifies with the pleasure the giantess experiences when crushing him.

Homosexuality	The man has an endosomatophilia fetish (eaten).
Dominated by a male	He becomes food for the giantess, dominated as an object.
Passive behavior	The giantess uses him.
Rejects his identity or sexuality	The giantess destroys him by chewing him.
Wishes to be a woman	By being ingested by the giantess woman, he becomes one with her.

Homosexuality	The man has a crush fetish.
Dominated by a male	He identifies himself with the object or bug being crushed by a giant female (male in disguise) and being dominated. The crushing is usually done in high heels, which are a subliminal phallic symbol.
Passive behavior	He is helpless in front of the large female
Rejects his identity or sexuality	The crushing destroys his identity.
Wishes to be a woman	Identifies simultaneously with the woman, the pleasure the woman exhibits, and at the same time with the bug being crushed

I will leave it to you to conduct the same analysis in some other forms of female domination fetishes such as coprophilia, trample fetish (another form of crush fetish), face sitting, and ass worshiping. I think that you begin to see the parallels here and understand that the assertion that many fetishes are disguised homosexuality is probably correct. The question then becomes why fetishes develop. If we look at the integration of the sense of self by different affective fuels, we see it as an answer for this behavior. The sense of self begins to be integrated by social and religious fuels at a very early age, probably at the level of the protoego. Social and religious fuels form the basis of the superego, the moral conscience in the Freudian model. The later fuels are the intellectual, material, and emotional-sexual fuels. If the desire for paternal affection in the form of homosexuality as an affective fuel of the emotional-sexual type is rejected by the social and religious fuels that integrated the sense of self earlier, the self would try to obtain it by a different mechanism—fetishism, which is not as overt as homosexuality. This allows a fetish to bypass the filters of social and religious fuels, which integrated the sense of self at an earlier age. This earlier integration of the self is deeper since it is more ingrained in the sense of self. In addition, religious fuel, by promising an afterlife, counteracts the fear of nonexistence, so it has a lot of power in integration of the ego. Though homosexuality may be socially or religiously rejected, fetishes, which aren't overtly homosexual, can bypass social and religious fuels and allow the affective need of paternal or maternal affection that the sense of self still requires for integration. Homosexuals are looking for paternal affection. They learn to be submissive to gain this affection as a way for the self to survive. Now you begin to see why the universal fear of nonexistence and the need for integration with affective fuels beautifully explains the relationship between homosexuality and fetishism.

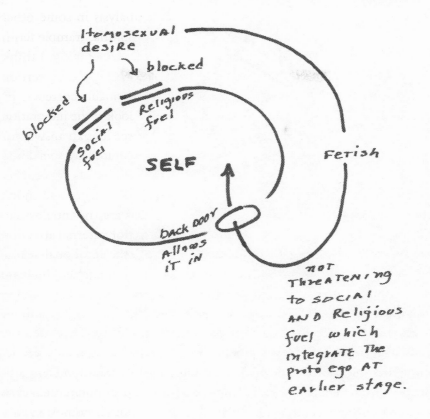

Let us examine bisexuality from the perspective of affective fuels and the process of identification. The male bisexual is essentially homosexual. When he is with another man, he is passive, and when he is with a woman, the predominant process is that of identification with the woman, as she experiences pleasure with him. By identifying himself with the woman, he is in essence reacting through her with a man, himself. In essence, by being passive with a man or identifying with a woman, he is exhibiting homosexual behavior.

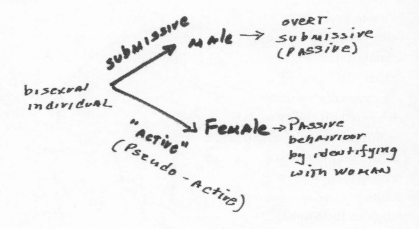

In view of the mechanisms of homosexuality, one has to pause before passing judgment on homosexuals. If it is genetic, it is beyond their control, and passing judgment on them would be akin to passing judgment on people based on their race. Whether it is genetically or psychologically acquired or even acquired by itself, it occurs at a very early age, during the development of the protoego, by a developing, immature self trying to deal with the fear of nonexistence. At this age, people have no control or knowledge of what is happening to them, so it is not morally correct to judge them for trying to survive in very adverse circumstances. Any one of us faced with this situation would probably wind up the same. Rehabilitation or conversion therapy tries to revert individuals to their natural sexuality, but it is successful approximately only a third of the time. Another third of those who undergo this therapy becomes asexual, and the last third remains the same. The reason for this success rate, I suspect, is that the therapy needs to do nothing less than completely break down and brainwash the individual, which is very painful and costly and can take years. I suspect that those people who are "cured" were able to substitute one of the other affective fuels for the emotional-sexual fuel as a mechanism of ego integration to complete the transformation.

Those who become asexual due to therapy probably do so because they reject the emotional-sexual fuel through the social and religious fuels' filters but are not able to substitute the emotional-sexual fuel with another fuel as a mechanism for ego integration. Thus, they become psychically castrated by religious and social fuels. A patient once explained to me how he was very close to realizing his natural sexuality and accepting it by substituting intellectual fuel for emotional-sexual fuel. He began reconstructing a sense of self on his intellectual achievements. In the process, he suffered severe emotional distress that hampered his ability to continue the substitution of intellectual fuel for emotional-sexual fuel as a mechanism of ego integration. He reverted to utilizing emotional-sexual fuel as a mechanism of integration and reverted to homosexuality. Those who remain the same are unable to substitute one fuel for another and do not have the filter of social and religious fuels to block overt homosexuality. It is for this reason that I believe we must pause before passing judgment on these individuals; they are human beings, children of God, faced with an adverse environment. The sense of self had to do what it needed to do to survive and integrate itself. If I, a simple human being, can understand this mechanism, how could God not understand it? Anyone who thinks ego restructuring is easy should test that belief. In Buddhist monasteries, the pinnacle of Japanese efficiency, Zen monks struggle for years, even decades, with affective fuels to reach *kensho* or *satori*, but only a few succeed. This process of rehabilitative or conversion therapy would be the equivalent in homosexuals of restructuring the ego at an emotional-sexual fuel level. Easy? Food for thought. We need to be compassionate with homosexuals and they with heterosexuals. Recently, a homosexual couple was ejected from a restaurant, but rather than getting angry, they were understanding and forgiving to the owner. I ask, who exhibited a more Christian attitude?

Another concept that needs to be discussed is that of sadomasochism. Sadomasochistic males want to be punished, dominated, and passive because of a subconscious desire to be a woman. Observe here that the contraction of the self through humiliation is self-imposed. Sadomasochistic males deny and destroy their sexuality. The self-imposed contraction of the self is associated with sex as a way of obtaining pleasure from ego contraction. Normally, this is painful. When the ego expands, it is pleasurable. For example, when we receive compliments, we feel elated. Our egos expand and feel less threatened by nonexistence. When people are humiliated, they feel they are less, their egos contract, and they feel threatened by nonexistence. When someone makes love with another, his or her ego expands, which reaffirms the sense of self. However, with the masochist, this pattern is reversed. Since he denies his sense of identity, he wishes to be protected and dominated, and the process of ego contraction during sex becomes pleasurable by deriving the acquisition of an alternative affective fuel to give the ego assurance in another realm. For example, he may accept pain (physical -material fuel) in exchange for emotional fuel. Thus, pain becomes pleasurable inasmuch as it is the way of obtaining another form of affective fuel to integrate the self. Egos thus can expand or contract in the sexual act. Since the necessity to feel dominated or obtain paternal affection is integrated earlier than other affective fuels, this overrides the sense of ego expansion based on other affective fuels and associates the ego contraction with obtaining affection and thus security. In the case of the female masochist, the security stems from feeling an extreme form of domination by the male so that she becomes like a child being punished by a paternal figure. In the case of the sadist, the sense of ego expansion of pleasure comes from experiencing the feeling of dominating another person and thus being in control. This grants the self a sense of security since it is controlling and determining what affective fuels the sadist wants. This causes ego expansion in the regular way, and when associated with sex, it can become pleasurable. The possibility also exists that the sadist may identify with the masochist. In this case, he experiences pleasure by exerting control and thus expanding his ego by identifying with the masochist if he himself has some masochist tendencies. I suspect, however, that in the case of the sadist, the element of control and ego expansion predominates. So ego expansion and contraction, which normally elicit pleasure and pain, respectively, can be reversed. Normally, one associates ego expansion with the sexual act as a pleasurable experience and establishes a sexual reflex with ego expansion. However, when the reverse happens and the ego contraction is associated with the sexual act, the reflex is inverted. This occurs because the need for paternal affection or domination was integrated at an early age, and the self learned to be passive or active depending on the situation as a survival mechanism. If ego contraction and being submissive were associated with receiving affection from a dominant, threatening figure, this survival pattern became ingrained early on. With puberty, the association of being submissive or ego contraction with sex takes place, and thus the person becomes excited with this particular behavior. The submissive behavior then guarantees the person affection, which he uses to integrate the self against nonexistence in spite of ego contraction from another angle. In other words, the ego may be willing to suffer a contraction in one aspect of itself if, on the other hand, it experiences an expansion in another aspect or with a different affective fuel. Which fuel the ego is willing to trade depends mostly on which fuel is more intrinsically linked to its early integration or which fuel is more easy to acquire in bigger quantities (affective fuel quantification). This ego contraction may occur in social fuel rather than the emotional-sexual affective fuel. It may also happen that the affection received at a primitive level such as a child would receive integrates the self at a deeper level at the expense of the affective fuels acquired later. Remember that before puberty, affection was the direct fuel of the sense of self for the child. At about puberty, a transition begins; children seek to obtain affective fuels independent of their parents as a way of reaffirming control and existence. If the need for this paternal and maternal affective fuel hasn't been met at the time of puberty, the adolescents may, as a survival mechanism, try to obtain it the old-fashioned way—by being submissive rather than by replacing it with other affective fuels. They in essence become stuck at a more primitive level of integration of the self and are unable to transition to utilizing the five affective fuels to integrate the sense of self. This ego contraction–pleasure reversal may be the basis for this mechanism. Sex then becomes the mechanism whereby this becomes a reflex that triggers excitement in these individuals since they have already associated it with ego contraction.

No discussion of fetishes would be complete without grappling with the crime of pedophilia. Pedophilia can cause profound physical and psychological damage in a child as well as strip the child of a sense of innocence. I suspect pedophiles look for affection from paternal figures by identifying with children. In the sexual act, they are concentrating on what the child feels, thus becoming like a child, who normally receives affection from parents. Pedophiles look to regress to a childlike state to receive that parental affection. The problem is that, as opposed to adult relationships, children have no say in the relationship and are profoundly damaged psychologically and physically by it. In short, the children become objects of the pedophiles' identification, devoid of any humanity. This is a profound crime. The adults in these cases already have poor social and religious filters that have failed to block this behavior. It is open to argument whether this lack of filters is due to circumstances beyond pedophiles' control, but there has to be a line between right and wrong and a profound awareness even without religion and social filters that damage is being done to another human being. It is easy to relativize all behavior by the concept of social and religious fuels, arguing that if you don't have the fuel integrated into your self by circumstances beyond your control, you're not responsible for your behavior. The problem with this is that at some point there has to be a recognition that damage is being done to the other person. That's why, instead of defining *good* and *evil* in terms of socially accepted or rejected behavior, I prefer to define *evil* as that which closes you off from the divinity of God or the absolute in another person. I define *good* as that which opens you to the divinity in the other. The absence of a social or religious fuel is no excuse for evil when free will and reasoning are present. The problem with pedophiles is that even though they are lacking social and religious fuels that will tell them this is wrong, they have structured their egos mostly on emotional-sexual fuel. This has the effect of encysting the ego to the point of not being able to recognize the humanity and fragility of children. It may also be that pedophiles have structured their sense of self mostly on a social or religious belief that allows for this behavior. This also encysts the ego and prevents them from recognizing the humanity of children.

Mechanism of Autophagia

Many individuals suffer from a condition known as autophagia, which may include variations of chewing the nails, trichophagia, and trichotillomania. Underlying many of these disorders are several common factors.

- An insecurity of the sense of self desires to be reinforced.

- The act of ingesting part of oneself such as trichophagia fills that necessity of self-assurance by two possible mechanisms.
- The act of pulling on the hair or actually feeling the sensation of biting on oneself is a form of self-stimulation that reinforces the sense of self. It reinforces the statement, "If I am feeling something, I must be existing."
- The act of ingesting something is equivalent to self-gratification, which psychologically tends to fill the sense of emptiness in the individual.
- By ingesting part of oneself, one reinforces the sensation of self because, after all, one is ingesting a part of oneself, therefore reinforcing the "sense of self."

A variation of this is cannibalism. A possible mechanism for cannibalism is based on the mechanism of identification. These people desire to be like the individuals they are ingesting because they feel that becoming like them will increase their sense of existence. Many primitive tribes believed that eating the hearts of their enemies would confer to them attributes that they admired in those individuals. In modern-day cannibalism, the predominant drive is a mechanism of identification with the individuals that the cannibals desire to eat. The underlying drive behind this is again a profound fear of nonexistence and the cannibal's belief that by eating the object of their identification, they will be more. As we can see from prior examples, the underlying drive for many of these pathological behaviors resides at the very bottom in a profound fear of nonexistence, and the pathology that we see are mechanisms to try and overcome that fear and solidified the sense of self.

A common behavior seen in adolescence is trichotillomania, and a very common triggering factor is when adolescents brace their sense of self on an affective fuel that they have chosen for integration. If this fuel is threatened, they may resort to that behavior of trichotillomania in order to reaffirm the sense of self against the fear of losing that affective fuel. For example, if a high school student is basing her sense of self on obtaining good grades, she realizes or reinforces the sense of self on the intellectual fuel. Faced with an exam that may result in success or failure (a good grade or a bad grade), the student may feel the fear of losing the intellectual affective fuel if she fails the exam. Since her sense of identity is based on obtaining a good grade, this presents the threat of lack of acquisition if she fails. At that point, the sense of self will resort to another mechanism to reinforce its existence, a mechanism that doesn't depend on outside forces or outside circumstances and that the individual controls or is within her immediate control. Thus, she may resort to trichotillomania in order to alleviate the anxiety of obtaining a bad grade (loss of an affective fuel) and reinforce the self against this fear of becoming less, or nonexistent.

Mechanism of Postpartum Depression

The exact cause of postpartum depression is not well understood and may have both biochemical and psychological components. I will not address the biochemical components but stay mostly on the psychodynamics of the psychological components. If we examine the postpartum depression symptoms, we can get an idea on how a mechanism can be explained psychologically.

Postpartum depression symptoms may include the following: (obtained from several sources)

- depressed mood or severe mood swings
- crying
- difficulty bonding with the baby
- withdrawal from family and friends
- anorexia or overeating
- inability to sleep or sleeping too much
- reduced interest in activities
- fatigue or loss of energy
- fear of not being a good mother
- feeling of worthlessness or guilt
- decreased ability to interact with others
- severe anxiety
- harming herself or the baby
- recurrent thoughts of death or suicide

We can begin to understand many of the symptoms from the perspective of affective fuels. Some of the symptoms can be triggered by the loss of affective fuels, and still other symptoms are compensatory mechanisms. First, let us analyze how the loss of affective fuels can trigger the symptoms.

During the pregnancy, the woman has the initial excitement of the pregnancy, and this results in increased attention, which is basically sublimated affection. At the same time, there is an experience of profound union with the baby in the womb. After the delivery, the realization comes that the woman now has to stop looking for affective fuels to integrate her sense of self and has to start living for another being, the baby. All of a sudden, the responsibility of providing for a creature hits home. The attention that the pregnant woman received initially eventually fades away, and the reality of caring for a baby every day sets in. Necessarily, the mother has to stop trying to acquire affective fuels for herself and has to start giving them to the baby. The delivery itself creates an anatomic fragmentation of union that also has psychological components, and this contributes to the symptoms. Understanding this, we can start to see how some of the symptoms begin to develop. The depression, or at least the psychological part of it, may result from the realization that the woman begins to lose the expectation of obtaining affective fuels of integration due to her responsibility of caring for a baby. She now faces some degree of isolation since she has to stay at home, she has to negate herself some material pleasures that she may have experienced before, she begins to use some of the morning to take care of the baby and not herself, and intellectually she may experience a loss of stimulation due to the interaction with a not-yet-fully-developed baby who operates at a very basic level.

As we can see, after the delivery the mother is faced with a loss of several affective fuels. More importantly, there is loss of hope of obtaining them in the immediate future, which can lead to a depression. This depression manifests itself as reduced interest and pleasure in activities, irritability due to the inability to obtain affective fuels, anxiety due to the lack of affective fuels, and crying, which is a manifestation of the loss of an affective fuel. The association of the loss of an affective fuel and the birth of the baby may lead to difficulty bonding with the baby since, subconsciously, the mother may blame the baby for the loss of affective fuels because of that attention the baby now requires. This may also explain thoughts of harming oneself or the baby.

On the other hand, after the delivery, the mother may sense fragmentation of union that may lead to symptoms of worthlessness, change guilt, or inadequacy and fears that the individual is not a good mother. Likewise, the subconscious blaming of the baby for the loss of affective fuels may also contribute to the sense of shame, guilt, and anger. The symptoms in the previous paragraph are primary symptoms of the loss of affective fuels; some of the other symptoms that a mother may experience are actually compensatory mechanisms for this loss. For example, overeating or sleeping too much may be a form of self-gratification as a mechanism for obtaining self-induced affection. The individual may resort to different forms of self-gratification in order to compensate for the loss of affective fuels due to the increased responsibility of having to care for a baby. These psychological symptoms may be exacerbated by the mother's hormonal and biochemical changes, which will exaggerate the response to the loss of affective fuels. So as we can see, some of the symptoms of postpartum depression are primary, and others are compensatory mechanisms. If the individual sees the pregnancy as a culmination of the love between two people, is able to transcend the need for self-affection, and begins to feel the underlying union with the child, the individual will have a normal postpartum reaction. If, on the other hand, the pregnancy is a mechanism to obtain attention or the individual is very dependent on attention, then the pregnancy may trigger postpartum depression after the delivery.

CHAPTER 4

Polarization by Social Fuel

Gratitude is what makes what we have enough.

—Unknown

A BUDDHIST STORY recounts a very fearsome samurai who was once told about a very pious monk. He went to see the monk, found him meditating in a lotus position, and asked him a question. "What is the difference between hell and heaven?"

The monk, without moving, replied, "Someone like you will never understand the difference." The samurai took this as an offense, unsheathed his sword, raised it, and prepared to strike the monk's neck. The monk said, "That is hell." The samurai hesitated and, after a few minutes of thinking, slowly sheathed his sword. He remained silent for a while, staring at the monk, and finally bowed to him. "That is heaven," said the monk.

As I mentioned before, the polarization we are seeing now in society is based on the five affective fuels of ego integration. In this chapter, we will discuss polarization by social fuel.

To begin, we must understand that there are different subsets of social fuel. Polarization can take place, not only on the main fuel itself but also on the different subsets. We are witnessing conflicts between Democrats and Republicans, between African-Americans and whites, between different nations, between fans of different sports affiliations, and between members of different ethnic communities.

Recently, a Republican congressman was shot by a member of the Democratic Party. Abraham Lincoln was shot by an individual with opposing viewpoints. More recently, death threats have been leveled against members of Congress and families to a degree that has never been seen before. Where does all this hate come from?

To begin to understand, we need to comprehend two factors. The first factor we need to consider is the mechanism of identification. The individual will tend to identify with a group of individuals who share the same affective fuels of ego integration. This, as I have explained before, affects the survival of the species by allowing sharing of common affective fuels that facilitate specific behavior patterns and cohesion within the group. When the group itself is threatened, the individuals would also be threatened on the respective fuel of integration that they share with the group. This will make the group of individuals come together to defend the group and, respectively, their own affective fuels. The individual who recently shot a congressman in the United States did so because he felt threatened in his affective fuels by the ideology of the congressman. He was probably integrated mostly on the social fuel—that is, his Democratic values—and lacked other venues of integration. He had "all the eggs in one basket," as the common saying goes. When people are integrated mostly on one affective fuel, their sense of self destabilizes quickly when this affective fuel is threatened. This quick destabilization is a profound threat to the sense of self and leads to violence. If the individuals had had other affective fuels to fall back on, the destabilization would not have been as profound and violence may have been averted.

The second factor we need to consider is that the driving force behind this violence is fear of nonexistence. If this fear did not exist, the individual would not feel that he is less when his social values are threatened by outside forces, and there would be no reason to respond with violence.

In summary, we have an individual who is mostly integrated on one affective fuel and who identifies with the group that shares those affective fuels that feels threatened when the values of that group are also threatened by a different ideology or affective fuel. Since this integration is mostly on one affective fuel, it is very threatening to the sense of self to lose it, and in order to avoid a profound ego contraction the person responds with violence. The driving force is again fear of nonexistence.

The power of this affective fuel of ego integration can be seen in the level of animosity between Democrats and Republicans. Both groups feel that their affective fuels are threatened by the other group and react with animosity. From the practical point of view, there is really no significant difference between a Republican and a Democrat. Both are bound by their own respective affective fuels, which they feel will make them "be more" in terms of material, intellectual, religious, or social fuels. Consider the Antifa movement, which is supposed to be antifascist (hence the name *Antifa*) and yet uses violence and intimidation to accomplish its goals—typical fascist behavior. They use violence because they themselves feel threatened in their integrative fuels by conservative values. The Antifa movement is based on the teaching of Herbert Marcuse, who taught that tolerance toward all viewpoints should be abandoned: "Tolerance cannot be indiscriminate and equal with respect to the content of the expression, neither in word or in deed; it cannot protect false words and wrong deeds which demonstrated that they contradict and counteract the possibilities of liberation." a quote attributed to Marcuse. Marcuse himself was bound by the affective fuels of ego integration, and he never saw past them. And although he talks about liberation, he refers to the exchange of one affective fuel for another. He is neither original in his thinking nor deep. He is just another philosopher staring at the branches of the tree without looking at the root of the behavior or understanding it. He segregates people on the basis of their affective fuels without understanding the unitive factors in all human beings. On the other hand, we have the alt-right, which is also feeling threatened in their values (think "affective fuels of ego integration") by the liberal mind, and they many times also respond with exclusion and prejudice. Both groups are governed by the same primal fear. Both groups respond with aggression to the fear without understanding the actual cause of it.

An example of this conflict is what happened in Charlottesville, Virginia, in August 2017 because of a statue. For the white supremacists who were there, the statue of a Southern general represented an element of ego integration and thus of self-identity. This was most likely secondary to a learned social fuel. The loss of the statue represented a loss of social fuel and an ego contraction threatening their identity.

To the Antifa group, the same statue represented a loss of social fuel and an ego contraction since it reminded them of a hurtful past. What represented a sense of identity for one group represented a loss of identity for the other group. Both groups were fighting for a social fuel to maintain their sense of identity through ego integration. Neither group realized the mechanisms in operation that were controlling their actions. Both groups were slaves to that primary fear of nonexistence and were controlled by it without realizing it. Rather than fighting each other over a symbol of integration, it would have been more productive and liberating, as well as constructive, for both groups to engage in a frank conversation about their fears and realize that they both share the same needs of ego integration and affection.

The conservative mind tends to conserve standard fuels of ego integration, while the liberal mind tends to try to liberate itself from the standard fuels and look for new ones as mechanisms of integration. Both, however, are bound by the mechanisms of integration, and there is no significant paradigm shift in the way of thinking between them.

The so-called liberal mind, if left to itself, would throw society into chaos. The reader may look for an example of this in some countries in South America that are governed by a liberal ideology. Riots are the order of the day, and daily demonstrations, bloodshed, and economic chaos are commonplace. On the other hand, the conservative mind, left to itself, would throw the country into stagnation. Again, the reader may look for examples of this in some countries and kingdoms in the Middle East, where societal advances and technological development are very limited and mostly dependent on outside sources. What both the liberal and conservative minds fail to realize is that they need each other. It is the interplay between these two sources that allows for the progression and development of society. The conservative mind helps to stabilize society so that, in the framework of a stable platform, the liberal mind can then develop new ideas. Shielded precisely by the stability in society, new ideas can be tested and then expanded without the danger of major changes that may imperil the society. The change occurs slowly and progressively. Forcing the change abruptly would throw the society into chaos and would be counterproductive. Both forces need each other in order for society to progress. It would be worthwhile for both groups of individuals to recognize their own humanity in each other and recognize the fear that governs them both. Change is necessary and is the only constant in the universe, but even nature brings change around at a slow pace, many times by trial and error and in small quantities, so as not to wipe out a complete species. Consider the dinosaurs and the comet strike (abrupt change) versus the genetic evolution of species (slow change).

Recognizing their mutual fear and understanding that it is the common denominator may help these divergent groups work together in a framework of respect and cooperation. This brings to mind a quote from a leader whom I respect and admire profoundly, Martin Luther King Jr.: "Love is the only force capable of transforming an enemy into a friend." This can be understood only once we realize that the true definition of *love* is the profound realization of your own true self in the other person (the concept of Union).

Another form of polarization is nationalism. Some quotes attributed to Albert Einstein about patriotism indicate that he did not hold it in very high regard. The culture of an individual is made up of the different affective fuels of integration. The social fuel, for example, may encompass aspects of language, style of dress, architecture, social interaction, education, food, and marriage. The religious fuel encompasses the religious belief systems and is self-explanatory. The intellectual fuel mostly deals with education and, to some degree, social interaction, while the material fuels deals with the economy of the particular culture and also with social interaction up to a point. The emotional-sexual fuel has to do with family relations and the interpersonal relationships between couples. It seems appropriate, however, to discuss nationalism under the heading of social fuel since it encompasses many of the other fuels that form a culture. As we can see, culture is mostly based on the different affective fuels, and when individuals feel that some or all of their affective fuels are threatened or challenged, they themselves will feel threatened in the concept of the self and will react aggressively toward the perceived threat. What the patriots of the various countries and nationalities fail to see is that the different affective fuels that compose the culture are learned behaviors that can be modified as needed. People will swear allegiance to a specific nation or country because they feel integrated on the specific affective fuels of that particular country despite never questioning whether those particular fuels of integration actually help them to grow as individuals. The loyalty of communists to their social fuel is as valid as the loyalty of democrats (referring to the general term, not the party term) to their social fuel. Both are integrated on the respective fuels and derive a sense of self from this integration. Both firmly believe in their respective fuels since they provide and afford them a sense of self.

What they are both deriving by this mechanism is a sense of existence or identity to protect themselves from the fear of nonexistence. What they both fail to realize is that their integration into these fuels occurred at an early age, at which they had no control, and for this reason they feel very threatened when these fuels are threatened. This occurs at the level of the protoego and solidifies the protoself at a very early age. Any attempt to change this fuel will be met with significant resistance since it directly threatens the sense of existence. We need to start realizing that the mechanisms of integration can be substituted for different ones and that the main reason for this substitution should be the benefit of humankind and nature.

Polarization by Social Credit

Another form of social polarization is taking place under the guise of social credit. In China, for example, this concept is being developed to monitor people's ways of thinking, searches on the Internet, purchases, and programs they listen to. If these things do not conform to the ideology of the government, the people are prevented from traveling or buying tickets to go abroad; suffer economic damages designed to make them bankrupt, as one Chinese official stated; and are prevented from pursuing higher education. This in turn prevents them from making a living because they cannot obtain jobs due to their lack of education, and it also prevents them from forming families since they cannot afford them. In essence, the government is denying these individuals the social, material, emotional-sexual, and intellectual fuels and the means to feel the unity that every human being craves. This is manipulation and polarization by social credit, although it impacts the other fuels. It is intended to homogenize the way people think by threatening the affective fuels of integration under the false assumption that this will prevent conflict and maintain the government in power. What they do not realize is that they are stagnating the mechanisms of social evolution by limiting the affective fuels that the sense of self uses for integration. As society evolves, the sense of self will try to obtain the different fuels of ego integration because it evolves also. When the acquisition of new affective fuels is blocked, the sense of self will look for alternative fuels of ego integration, and when it cannot obtain it, the self will become unstable and fall into social disorder. It is the equivalent of putting a lid on a kettle to prevent smoke from escaping without putting out the fire. This will work as long as the individual has a sense of self and desires affective fuels, but once the individual gives up hope of obtaining affective fuels or loses the sense of self, this mechanism of control ceases to be effective. In other words, the Chinese government is manipulating people through the fear of nonexistence by threatening the affective fuels that integrated the sense of self against this fear. A more effective way of bringing about the unity that they desire would be for the individual citizens to fully realize the unity that they have with one another. That only comes from the profound realization of the oneness that we all share, which transcends national identity. Compare the motivation of Mother Teresa of Calcutta, who gave her life to help others, with the motivation and ideology that forces you to help people. There is a profound difference. The problem with this approach of punishing people through the affective fuels in order to change their behavior is that it tends to marginalize groups of people. Once this group that has been marginalized is large enough, it will coalesce precisely because of the common factors. It will then turn against the government and destabilize it. So, in effect, if intervention is intended to marginalize a group of individuals, the actual effect is the opposite over the long term. It would be better if the people were educated through introspection so that they realized the city's duty and the responsibility that they have to one another. In this way, the change is not imposed from the outside in but from the inside out.

Another form of polarization we are sadly seeing is polarization by race. The African-American community has suffered discrimination and prejudice unjustly for many years. It took the likes of a moral giant in the person of Martin Luther King Jr. to bring the white community to realize that prejudice. Although steps still have to be taken to continue to eradicate prejudice, it is unfortunate that some in the African-American community as well as in the white community have tended to isolate themselves from one another by taking refuge in the solidification of the self, hiding themselves behind the affective fuels that constitute a sense of identity. We see, for example, a reaffirmation of the "whiteness" of a group of individuals by advocating membership in the Ku Klux Klan. On the other hand, there is also a reaffirmation of the African-American identity by some groups such as Black Lives Matter, which in some cases has advocated for violence against police officers. Both groups feel threatened by the other because their sense of identity is threatened, and this leads to a polarization by identifying themselves with the group they feel protects their affective fuels as mechanisms of ego integration. There is no significant difference at the very bottom between the groups. Both are governed by the same fear of nonexistence and rely on identification with their respective groups in order to protect their affective fuels of ego integration. A profound transformation has to take place in the individuals of each respective group so that they can start seeing the humanity in one another. Both groups are subject to the fear of nonexistence and, predictably, look for safety by identifying themselves with the groups that protect their affective fuels.

At this point it is worth asking the question why there is a surge in violence and intolerance in our society. We live in a society that, when compared to other societies in the world, provides for almost everything a person will need. Yet we seem to be asking for more, never satisfied. Several mechanisms appear to be operating that increase this polarization from the point of view of social affective fuel.

Increased Population Density

Increased population density worsens polarization by bringing into close contact different groups with opposing affective fuels. For example, a group of individuals may derive its sense of identity from the ethnic social fuel, but within that group may be individuals who have opposing political views. Since people tend to group together to feel safe in this sense of identity, this brings different groups into conflict from the perspective of their political views. Observe that within the social affective fuel category, you may have subsets that oppose one another. A denser population may also bring polarization due to competition for different affective fuels and increase the amount of interaction between different groups, whereas before, groups that were perhaps miles or towns apart now may be within the same city and even within the same block.

Increased Communication

A century ago what happened in another continent would not be heard of in another country for weeks or months due to the distances and methods of communication, but now what happens in another continent is at our fingertips in a matter of seconds or minutes due to electronic communication. This makes the conflicts among different affective fuels surface almost immediately since they appear to more directly affect us.

Polarized Media

It is well known that there is a profound polarization in the media that fans the fires of polarization among different groups. Due to the quick communication, what used to be localized to a small town or city now becomes known worldwide in a matter of minutes. You can get the latest news from Britain, France, Germany, and African countries just by browsing the Internet or cable news.

The Advent of Social Media

Social media allows for communication to take place without facing any other person. This tends to dehumanize people you're communicating with because there is no face-to-face interaction. It is very easy to block someone on Facebook or Twitter by just pressing a button. Also, because of the wide reach of social media, what used to be a conflict limited to a few individuals now becomes widespread. Observe, for example, the phenomenon of cyberbullying, which can result in an individual being destroyed in days. There is an increased dependency on social media and acceptance by those on it as a mechanism of ego identity. For example, people may feel that their worth is determined by how many likes they get on Facebook. Thus, a widespread rejection on Facebook may have devastating consequences for them.

Convergence and Divergence

Do understand this concept: we can look at the development of language as an example of convergence and divergence. As primitive humans began to spread from their birthplace into different parts of the world, migration of a group of individuals or tribes to a new location would take weeks if not months, and the communication with the original tribe that was left behind was difficult and at times impossible due to the distances. The protolanguage that developed within the original tribe was likely modified by the migrating tribe, with new words developed to describe the environment and interactions. The language took a divergent path from the original language, which probably resulted in the different languages that we have now.

Presently, because of the advances in communication and transportation, a trip that would have taken months in times past takes only hours now. This brings together different cultures, different ideas, and different affective fuels, which can lead to conflicts. In effect, whereas there was a divergence of ideas and cultures in earlier times, now there is a convergence of those ideas and cultures due to improved communication and transportation. This exposure to other ideas and cultures creates conflicts by bringing various affective fuels into conflicts with one another. Individuals derived their sense of identity from the different affective fuels, and they will try to protect those fuels to maintain their sense of identity. Witness, for example, the conflict between China and the United States in which each country is trying to promote its culture as a mechanism of preserving its sense of identity. What they do not realize is that this sense of identity is a learned behavior and that if we are going to survive as a species we will have to transcend this. This will be difficult. Attempts by European countries to integrate large immigration groups are running into problems precisely because of the conflicts among different affective fuels. The shock of cultures is really a shock of affective fuels. Each group of people fights to maintain and increase their affective fuels against the other groups.

So far we have been discussing macropolarization from the social point of view. It so happens that micropolarization also exists from the affective social fuel. An example of this can be seen in the conflict between adolescents and parents. During the adolescent years, the parents provide the five affective fuels of ego integration to their adolescent children. They are sheltered (material fuel), they're members of the family (social fuel), they're given a religious education (religious fuel), they are given affection and may have a girlfriend or boyfriend (emotional-sexual fuel), and they are getting an education (intellectual fuel), which may or may not be paid for depending on whether they go to public school or private school, but even then, some degree of financial support is always present. Adolescents begin to realize they are dependent on the five affective fuels of ego integration and that this dependency can end if the family members die off or disappear. The adolescents feel the need to establish control over the affective fuels that they use to integrate themselves so that if their families disappear, they are not left without those affective fuels. They try to look for them outside the family nucleus, and in so doing, they react with hostility and sometimes even aggression toward the family because they may feel that the family is hindering their attempts to obtain affective fuels by themselves—in other words, that they are hindering the adolescents' ability to establish control over the affective fuels that they need independent of the family. If the family offers help and encouragement in the effort to obtain the affective fuels and become independent, the adolescents sense that they're not trying to control them and become less hostile. If, on the other hand, the family tries to control their lives, even out of concern for their welfare, without understanding that they're trying to establish control over their affective fuels, then this would trigger more aggression and hostility on the part of the adolescent. This is the reason that many adolescents are so rebellious toward their parents. In essence, they are afraid of losing the affective fuels that have always been provided by them and, sensing a dependency on them, try to obtain their own affective fuels to feel more secure. This is an example of micropolarization.

Gangs

Another example of micro-polarization is gangs. A gang, in essence, provides young adolescents, who are trying to obtain independence from their families, with all the affective fuels of ego integration. For example, they provide social fuel in the form of acceptance, material fuel in the form of money from drugs, intellectual fuel in the form of learning illicit ways to make money, religious fuel in the sense of loyalty or adherence to the group, and finally emotional-sexual fuel by providing interaction between the sexes and many times treating members of the opposite sex as objects. This adherence to the gang leads individuals to defend the affective fuels by committing actual violence if the gang requires it to maintain membership. The gang in essence becomes a mini country with its own rules and regulations and citizens who defend the affective fuels that give them a sense of identity contrary to other gangs with a different set of affective fuels.

The unification or coalescence of the gang has its beginning in the social and religious fuel. It makes sense because these two fuels are the first two fuels of ego integration at the level of the protoego. People tend to coalesce in terms of language and customs, which is the social fuel, and religious belief systems earlier than other fuels like the material, intellectual, and emotional-sexual fuel. Once this unification has taken place in terms of the social and religious fuels, then the gang begins to expand to obtain the other fuels—intellectual, material, and emotional-sexual, in that order. It is worth mentioning that individuals' acquisition of affective fuels follows a defined order. The first two fuels are the social and religious fuels obtained from the family, neighbors, and close friends, followed by education (intellectual fuel), a job (material fuel), and finally a family (emotional-sexual fuel). The gang pattern of unification or coalescence follows the same pattern. The initial two fuels in unification are the social and religious fuels because they are the ones that form the basis for the protoego, to develop a sense of self or identity. Once this is achieved, then the acquisition of the other affective fuels takes place and the process to obtain other fuels begins. The gang provides its members with a sense of identity by giving them a sense of respect, recognition, and identity, in that order. It is for this reason that individuals develop a quasireligious attachment or loyalty to the gang. This can be construed as being the religious fuel where the loyalty lies not to a deity but to the gang itself. Some give themselves name like "La Muerte," meaning "the death," which has semireligious connotations. As we can see, membership in gangs becomes a quasireligious experience and many times substitutes the religious belief system in a deity.

Conflicts between gangs are due not only to the acquisition of areas or turf, where a gang can operate and obtain material fuel, but also to concerns about recognition or identification with one gang or another. This is due to the fact that this recognition provides individuals with a sense of identity. Later, the conflict may involve different tactics (intellectual fuel) of obtaining the other affective fuels, eventually including the emotional-sexual fuel. One gang may strive to control members of the opposite sex for prostitution or for their own personal use. In short, the mechanism of gang operation mimics or is a microuniverse of the individual mechanism of integration. If a group of individuals in a society does not integrate it is due to either (1) mechanisms such as religious or social fuels, which may block integration by telling the individuals that if they integrate they may be condemned to go to hell or be rejected by their native society (think nonexistence) or (2) rejection of the individuals due to their cultural (social), religious, material, intellectual, or emotional fuel by the majority culture of a country, which makes individuals feel that they are "less" (again, think nonexistence).

Then, in order to maintain a sense of self-worth and existence against the primary fear of nonexistence, individuals drift into communities or groups of individuals that share the same affective fuels to maintain their sense of identity and integrity. Because the sense of identity begins at the level of the protoego, at a very early age, several steps must be taken in order to prevent this polarization and formation of cultural ghettos in different countries.

1. A common language has to be emphasized so that cross-cultural barriers can start to be breached.
2. Young individuals have to be educated that there is a common law for the country that makes everybody equal and that cannot be superseded by social or religious belief systems. This of course would be met with resistance from those already integrated.
3. Education should be compulsory so that individuals can start acquiring intellectual fuel and eventually material and emotional–sexual fuel to enable them to integrate into the community.
4. Attempts at self-segregation and establishment of laws and rules that are contrary to the host country or regional laws and rules have to be discouraged strongly.
5. Discrimination, either direct or reverse, has to be called out. Political correctness has to be thrown out the window when a group of individuals significantly harms or destroys other people's lives. This goes both ways. The same way that we cannot tolerate discrimination against a minority or harm against that minority, we also cannot tolerate that minority harming or discriminating against a majority. If calling out someone for harming another human being makes one a "racist," then not calling out someone for fear of being called a racist makes one a coward.

If left unfettered, the gangs will eventually coalesce into larger groups and create a country within a country, with higher degrees of polarization that eventually lead to civil war. We need to understand that people coalesce into groups in terms of affective fuels. With the advent of increased communication and travel, these affective fuels are being thrown into conflict with one another. Unless we're able to realize the relativity of these affective fuels and the mechanisms whereby they integrate the sense of self, the conflicts will only increase with time. In order to overcome these affective fuels, we need to understand in depth the need for them and the mechanisms by which they integrate the sense of identity. Understanding this, then, will lead to the realization that culture is essentially an accumulation of affective fuels that makes us feel comfortable in the face of the fear of nonexistence. Common ground has to be found with equal rights for everyone, regardless of religion, race, culture, economic status, and sexual orientation. Universal rights cannot be based on any religious belief system or social system that gives advantage to one group over another; they have to be universal. Individuals must be free to choose the religious belief systems that best suit their fear of nonexistence. If we fail to do this, the price that we will pay will be war.

Another example of micropolarization can be found in the effect of peer pressure on young people. With the advent of social media, a large number of young people have become dependent on their peers' acceptance. Whereas before, their interaction was limited to individuals or small groups, social media provides a much wider-reaching interaction. Instead of interacting with one or two people, people may be interacting with one or two hundred people simultaneously. They look for acceptance and approval from this group of people through social media (social fuel). When the group turns on and rejects them, they in essence lose a social affective fuel of ego integration. They sustain a profound ego contraction, feel more threatened by nonexistence, and may even commit suicide due to the pain they experience.

Another example would be the interaction in the office among different individuals who may have different loyalties to different bosses. They may reject one another and start petty grievances that may make the atmosphere in the office uncomfortable. The phenomenon of social media has accelerated and magnified the micropolarization process. One mechanism by which this happens is the anonymity that social media allows. Before it came along, the rejection of an individual would take place face to face, but now that rejection is faceless and can involve greater numbers of people. I am surprised by individuals who would not say insulting things to my face and yet would send them via e-mail or post them on social media. The anonymity shields them from rejection by the other person and is more bearable than a face-to-face interaction, where a rejection would be immediate and more profound.

All these conflicts are based on affective fuels. All of them obey a need for ego integration against this fear of nonexistence. The problem we have now is that these conflicts will continue to worsen due to the simultaneous increase in communication, which causes people to feel threatened by an affective fuel of another group that threatens their sense of identity. Howard Gardner, a professor of education at Harvard University, proposed that human beings possess different types of intelligence: musical-rhythmic, visual- spatial, verbal-linguistic, logical-mathematical, bodily-kinesthetic, interpersonal, intrapersonal, and naturalistic. All of them pertain to the exterior affective fuels, but the intrapersonal intelligence pertains to the mechanics of these affective fuels on ego integration. This is the one that explains the motivation, behavior characteristics, and sense of identity of individuals. We're going to have to develop the intrapersonal intelligence to understand the mechanisms of ego identity and the primal fear that governs the sense of self in order to be able to control our aggressive tendencies and survive as a species.

Aggressivity stems from individuals' feeling threatened in their sense of self by nonexistence because of the loss or lack of acquisition of an affective fuel, which leads to an ego contraction or lack of expansion and makes the ego more vulnerable to nonexistence. Any mechanisms that trigger this fear will trigger aggressivity.

When individuals are engaged in a discussion and their viewpoints are rejected or ridiculed, they may develop aggressivity. If the viewpoints are rejected solely on facts and not on a personal basis, the individuals may feel uncomfortable but not aggressive. The degree of ego contraction that they feel will not be so severe that they approach nonexistence. If, on the other hand, they are ridiculed, they take this as a more direct attack on their selves and the ego contraction is stronger. Now they feel much more threatened by nonexistence and becomes aggressive. A modulating factor on this response is how much the individuals have vested their sense of self in their opinions or work. For example, if a woman derives her sense of identity mostly from her political affiliation, a discussion with her about baseball in which her preference for a particular team is derided may lead to only a mild ego contraction because her sense of self or identity is not based on sports. If, on the other hand, her political views are ridiculed, the ego contraction will be stronger since her sense of identity is mostly based on them, and she would react with aggressivity and even violence. For an example of this, one only needs to look at the current state of politics in the United States, which would make any sane person cringe. In June 2017, a congressman and several other people were shot by an individual with a Democratic Party political affiliation. This individual most likely had his sense of self invested in his political views. The congressman, representing the Republican Party, threatened his sense of self with his viewpoints, and this led to aggressive behavior that resulted in violence. Think for a second about the degree of investment his sense of identity must have had in his political affiliation to lead him to commit an act of violence. The only logical explanation is that this individual's self felt threatened by the viewpoints of the other person. This threat was not physical but psychological. And it would only make sense if the psychological threat would lead to a profound ego contraction, which would then make the person feel more afraid of nonexistence and trigger aggressivity. If there is no fear of nonexistence, then a differing viewpoint would not threaten someone's sense of self to that degree. Only when there is an existential threat to an individual (in this case, not a physical threat where his life could be terminated, because obviously the congressman was not threatening him physically) from the point of view of ego or self existence will aggressivity develop. This only makes sense if the ego or self would feel threatened (by an ego contraction) by something. And this "something" has to be nonexistence.

Another concept that we need to understand is that of "power harassment." Power harassment occurs when one individual is in a higher position than another individual. The higher position affects that individual's behavior by integrating the sense of self and the newly acquired position. This leads to an ego expansion based on the new position of authority. When the individual exerts his or her authority over another person, this reaffirms his or her ego integration by reaffirming an ego expansion. The problem is that after each ego expansion, the fear of nonexistence reappears, leading to a need to reaffirm that authority again by exercising it over another individual. This leads eventually to power harassment, where the individual begins to abuse another person as a mechanism of ego expansion so that he or she feels secure against nonexistence. The mechanism of bullying is very similar. Through physical, intellectual, social, sexual or religious abuse, bullies exert control over other individuals, which reaffirms their sense of identity by the mechanism of ego expansion. The driving force is again the fear of nonexistence. After each event of bullying, the fear of nonexistence reappears, leading to another episode of bullying in an attempt to reaffirm the self against this fear. This is why it becomes a repetitive action.

There is an element of truth to the saying "Absolute power corrupts absolutely," and it has to do with the mechanism of ego integration. As the sense of self solidifies with different affective fuels, the fear of nonexistence becomes more acute. The more sense of self one has, the more it is exposed to the fear of nonexistence. At the same time, it becomes more alienated from the sense of union. The end result is that the sense of self requires an ever-increasing amount of affective fuels to feel safe against this primal fear, which necessitates the exercise of power to feel secure more and more frequently. The individual with such a solidified sense of self will see any attempt to undermine the affective fuels of ego integration as a direct threat to his or her existence, and his or her response will be ever more aggressive and more violent. This is the mechanism of dictators. This process accelerates as the ego becomes more solidified since it requires more and more affective fuels to maintain its integration. The opposite is also true. As the individual has less of a concept of self (for example, monks who strive to negate the sense of self), there is less need for affective fuels and the individual becomes more altruistic. The acceleration process also takes place in this group of individuals but it progresses toward a dissolution of the self. I briefly mentioned the sense of union and the need for it, but I will discuss this more in depth in terms of religious fuel, where I think it is more appropriately discussed.

Anatomy of Power

Why do people have power over other individuals? To understand the concept of power, one has to understand that it is based on the need for affective fuels. There is usually an individual who holds an affective fuel and another individual who desires or needs that affective fuel for integration. The first individual exerts his or her power through that affective fuel desired by the other individual. For example, the news from Hollywood in 2018 was about a producer who was accused of being a sexual predator by many aspiring actresses. How did this individual control so many women? To understand his power, one needs to understand that he was holding the social affective fuel of fame, riches, and money as a bargaining chip. On the other hand, the women desired to be famous and rich. They had a desire for social fuel that they thought would give them the emotional stability to feel secure against the fear of nonexistence. It is precisely because they desired this fuel so much that they were willing to put up with all the antics of the individual who held the ability to grant them that social fuel. As long as they had this desire, the individual would have power over them. An extreme case of this power is that of a dictator who holds the ability to terminate people's lives. Life in itself is a material fuel. As long as the people are afraid of losing their lives, they will acquiesce to the dictator's power. At some point, however, if they lose the fear of death, then the dictator ceases to exert control over them. This is what happened in Romania with a dictator who, after controlling the people for many years and making life unbearable for them, was toppled when the population lost the fear of death and rebelled against him. The same process took place with Muammar al-Qaddafi in Libya.

In both cases, one can see that the exercise of power is linked to either (1) the desire for an affective fuel of ego integration, such as fame and riches or (2) the fear of losing or loss of an affective fuel of ego integration (life, freedom), as explained in a prior chapter on the fear of ego contraction. But what effect does this power have on the individual who wields the power?

When individuals have absolute control over the affective fuels that integrate their sense of self or other people's sense of self, their sense of self undergoes a profound solidification. The solidification has, as a byproduct, a sense of alienation from the people around them, a sense of isolation, and an increase in the fear of losing those affective fuels. This is because the fear of nonexistence reappears after each integration, and the more sense of self one has, the bigger the fear gets. As the sense of self comes to rely more on more on the need for affective fuels to maintain its self integration, the fear of losing those fuels increases. This leads to the sense of self becoming more aggressive and despotic to try and maintain these fuels. As I explained before, after each exercise of power, there is a brief sense of integration that leads to people feeling more in control. The problem is, however, that the fear of nonexistence reappears and the individuals need to reassert the power. Each cycle of reasserting the power becomes more violent as individuals feel the inability to cope with the fear of nonexistence. One has to understand that there is no plateau or stable point. It is like being on top of a mountain and starting to accelerate in one direction or the opposite. The more sense of self the individual attains, the higher the dependency on affective fuels is, the greater the need to obtain them is, and the greatest the fear of losing them is. On the other hand, if people live in a monastery and begin to negate the self, the less they feel a need for integration and the less they are affected by the fear of nonexistence. The process will accelerate in one direction or the other but will not stay a on a stable point or a plateau.

Another subtle form of polarization is polarization by technology. A recent research study by Cigna health insurance company revealed an increased level of loneliness in the United States. Paradoxically, the advent of social media and technology has exacerbated the loneliness in people. By facilitating anonymity in social media, where individuals may reject or accept others by e-mail or blog comment without direct face-to-face contact, we have actually increased communication but at the same time, paradoxically, increased isolation. We are more connected technologically but more isolated socially and physically. Electronic interaction has replaced face-to-face interaction, and this has led to an increasing feeling of loneliness in individuals. People who are able to adapt to this type of communication are being separated or polarized from those who need human interaction to communicate. The net effect is a polarization in society in which large groups of individuals who lack technological adeptness are being marginalized from other groups, causing an epidemic of loneliness. Even among individuals who are technologically savvy, loneliness is beginning to creep in. Although technology increases communication at an intellectual level, it fails to bring about a sense of union because it lacks the physical contact that is necessary in human interactions. Try nurturing a baby with a computer instead of holding him and see what happens. We are programmed to have physical contact in our interactions with others. Technology has replaced this physical interaction and the nuances of our facial expressions, body language, physical touch, and other mechanisms with a purely intellectual communication. This lack of physical interaction, face-to-face communication, and social exposure contributes to this isolation even in an age of increased communication. Technology also further isolates individuals by facilitating the acquisition of material fuel in those who are more technologically educated. The sense of union is a spiritual characteristic that cannot be obtained by the distant communication afforded by technology. It comes about only through direct contact with another human being where all the senses that have been programmed into us by thousands of years of evolution come into play. Empathy comes around from seeing the suffering of others and by sharing their physical experiences and emotional pain—things that are difficult to transmit electronically.

Polarization by age is another form that corresponds to micropolarization. This is mostly seen in societies that are rather advanced and in which the elderly are relegated to nursing homes or assisted living facilities. This form of polarization is more subtle since it is not based on an antagonistic relationship. Nevertheless, it is a polarization in the sense that a separation takes place and society relegates these individuals to second-class citizens. In more primitive cultures, elderly people are respected and made to feel they are part of the family and society. In a highly technological society, however, due to their lack of technological literacy, they tend to fall behind, and in a subtle way they are consigned to nursing homes and assisted living facilities. Part of this polarization takes place because there is no common ground for communication between the elderly and the young people, but a more subtle reason may be that the elderly remind us of our future and the possibility of death (nonexistence) and we therefore tend to push them away from our conscious mind. Although no overt antagonism is present, nevertheless, there's the sensation of their being cumbersome and out of touch. Rarely are the elderly were come into a social event or intermingled with younger people. Part of the reason for this micro polarization may be that fear of eventually becoming like them (which we will) and thus the segregation is an attempt to put them behind us. It is cruel to see individuals that have contributed to the development of our society discarded to a nursing home or assisted living facility so that they do not interfere with the family life or social events. Only through the profound realization of the oneness that we share with them can we overcome our intrinsic prejudice of them and increase the social interaction with them. They may not be technologically advanced, and technically handicapped, however what they lack in technological prowess, they make up in wisdom. They have the ability many times to see things in their proper perspective, and to see things in the relative values. This is something that younger people usually lack due to lack of experience.

Micropolarization is also evident in polarization by weight. In our society, a very high importance is placed on being physically fit and slim. Overweight people are usually put down or embarrassed; consider, for example, the present modality of body shaming taking place in social media. One must question why these people are made to feel ashamed by those who possess a lean physique. Instead of being supportive, people tend to be cruel and offensive. Why? The reason lies in the fact that the slim individuals have a profound fear of becoming like the obese individuals (identification). Therefore, they reject the obese people by the same mechanism of prejudice explained before for fear of becoming obese themselves and losing the social and emotional as well as material affective fuels and "becoming less." This would make them feel more threatened by nonexistence. Their reaction is to be offensive to obese people and reject them to avoid the process of identification. It is true that obesity carries with it not only a social stigma but also a physical disadvantage since it is a risk factor for many types of diseases, including heart disease, cerebrovascular disease, hypertension, diabetes, and others. The problem is that instead of treating it and understanding it as a medical condition, society tends to give it a social stigma with the consequence of psychological rejection. In the Middle Ages, many paintings depicted rather plump and sometimes obese men and women. This was due to the fact that food was not readily available to poor people and obesity was associated with power, riches, and an increased chance of survival. The concept of beauty was probably associated more with a plump woman than with a slim woman at that time for those reasons. With increased food availability, however, that distinction disappears, and now, due to the presence of diseases and other factors, the stigma of obesity begins to arise.

As we can see, polarization is taking place within the set of social affective fuel and also in the different subsets of that same affective fuels. The mechanism for this polarization stems from the fact that the individuals will try to get a sense of identity through one of the subsets or sets of affective fuels. Due to the fear of becoming less by the process of identification with the other individual whose espouses a different affective fuel, the person tends to reject or block the other individual, and the polarization process begins. However due to the many subsets of affective fuels that there are, these multiply the possibilities for polarization can take place in society. All that is needed for this process to begin is a group of individuals integrating themselves on one particular affective fuel and another group of individuals espousing an opposite set of affective fuels.

These affective fuels that we are discussing affect not only individuals but also whole countries. For example, against all odds, Donald Trump was elected president of the United States. According to some authors in the Jewish press, the reason he was elected was George Soros. This is an interesting observation, allegedly from the *Jerusalem Post*. But how can this be? By all appearances, Soros and Trump are on opposite ends of the spectrum. But are they really? Let us start by analyzing Soros's motives. He appears to be a brilliant businessman and a compassionate philanthropist. The fact that he was exposed during his childhood to a fragmentation of society, where his own life and those of others were in danger, probably instilled in him a desire for union. He likely felt threatened by the polarization of society and the outright anti-Semitism exhibited by the Nazis. This relates to the concept of fragmentation of union as a cause of psychological pain explained in a prior chapter. In addition, he experienced the accumulation of power in a segment of society that represented the government, and this led him to distrust and established government because he probably saw it as a mechanism of control or oppression. Therefore, most likely his desire is to bring about the union of people through the homogenization of society. That is why he is for open borders and has thrown millions of dollars into promoting immigration into Europe and the United States.

Second, this massive immigration serves to dilute the power of and destabilize the government, which, as previously explained, Soros saw as a mechanism of oppression because of the accumulation of power in a segment of the population, which was then utilized for oppression. He wrote a book on reactive economics, but he himself is reacting psychologically to that fragmentation of union he experienced as a child. The problem with this approach is that he's throwing together individuals with different affective fuels. These individuals already are integrated on affective fuels that they learned during childhood at the level of the protoego. Many of these affective fuels block integration, precisely what he's trying to achieve. The net result is the polarization of society, to the point where Europe now has "no-go" zones; if you don't belong to a specific ethnic or religious group but enter a certain zone, you are in danger. Some of these affective fuels will tell individuals that they can be condemned to eternal hellfire if they accept democracy, while other affective fuels make individuals regard those from different ethnic groups as inferior or subhuman. Immigrants' rejection of the host culture, which they consider to be inferior, actually serves to polarize the host culture against them and intensify the polarization mechanisms. They essentially threaten the affective fuels of the host culture and thus cause the polarization. This attempt to homogenize society by immigration without regard for the affective fuels has counterproductive effects because, essentially, it brings together people with different affective fuels who feel threatened by one another. So although the intention is perhaps good, the net effect will be disastrous in many of the countries affected by this massive immigration. Several movements have now developed to emphasize the nationality and identity of the host country. In the United States, Barack Obama, as a liberal president, probably held the same views and pushed for immigration, a push that was helped by Soros's philanthropic donations. This caused the same effect as in Europe, where indigenous Americans felt threatened by individuals who wanted to reject the Christian beliefs and impose their own religious belief systems, which many times regarded those who did not believe like them as subhuman or inferior. The net effect was predictable. If there is such a thing as reactive economics, then there is also such a thing as reactive psychology—more precisely, reactive affective fuels. By advocating the values of the Native American population, Trump defended the affective fuels that constituted the identity of the American people. The fear of losing these affective fuels led the vote to go in favor of Donald Trump. He appears to be an individual who deeply cares about his country, has a good heart, and wants to defend his sense of identity. Although on the surface Soros and Trump appear to be worlds apart, both are governed by the same intrinsic fear of nonexistence. Their mechanisms of dealing with this fear are what differ. Soros likely was impacted by the fragmentation of union, which caused psychological pain and brought about the fear of ego contraction and the fear of nonexistence. His mechanism of dealing with this is bringing forth union by the homogenization of society. Trump wants to defend his affective fuels of identity and culture against the same fear, but his mechanism of defense is by reinforcing the social, material, religious, intellectual, and emotional-sexual fuels that compose his sense of identity as an American. In doing so, he also desires the union of the American people against what he sees as a force attacking their sense of identity. So in a way, through the process of reactive psychology (reactive affective fuels), Trump is the product of Soros. The funny part is that I think they both want the same thing. They both seem to be good individuals with their hearts in the right place. Instead of trying to force one mechanism of union over the other, what they should do is sit down, analyze the mechanisms of fragmentation and division, and devise a plan to work together toward the betterment of humanity. We have to understand that the sense of self is a mechanism of evolution by facilitating the adaptation to the environment through the process of identification of behavior change rather than genetics. In this manner, it is highly effective and quick in reacting to changes in the environment. At the same time, it is also very reactive to a threat against one of the affective fuels that compose its sense of identity. As long as we continue to hold the self as something solid, this will prevent us from seeing ourselves in another person and the fragmentation will continue. It is only when we deeply understand this mechanism that we have the courage to let go all the affective fuels and become "less," enabling ourselves to surpass these divisions and start working together toward the common good. That is a tall order. These concepts are hard to introspect and analyze, and it is even harder to let go of the affective fuels because of the threat we feel toward the sense of self. However, if we are to survive as a species, we must.

In March 2018, the very famous physicist Dr. Stephen Hawking passed away. He was a brilliant mind and a person worthy of the deepest admiration. He made several breakthroughs in physics and in science. He made a statement saying that if humanity is to survive, we should reach to the stars and plan to expand beyond our world. Although I agree this would be something desirable, I would argue that unless we learn to control and understand the sense of self first, we would take with us to the new world the same conflicts and polarization that we have here. It would be a matter of time before we were running into the same problems we have in this world, from the point of view of society and environment, in the new planets. So before we try to colonize new worlds, we must first try to understand the self and see the unity among us so that, together as humanity in a conjoined effort, we can reach for the stars. If instead of fighting one another, making nuclear weapons, and claiming that God loves one more than the other, we were to join forces, help one another out, and work together in science, imagine where we would be. We would be on Mars by now. If we are to survive as a species, we must first put a bridle on the sense of self and understand that it is just another mechanism of evolution. As a matter of fact, the only chance that we have to reach the stars within a reasonable amount of time—before a life extinction event takes place—is precisely to learn to work together and overcome our differences. We are responsible for one another.

Questions:

1. What are the social subsets of affective fuels that help you integrate or make you feel better? List them.
2. If you have an enemy, what are the subsets of social affective fuels that integrate him or her? List them.

3. Can you see the similarities between the subsets of affective fuels that you have and your enemy has? List them.

4. What are your fears, and how do they relate to the social affective fuels? List them.

5. What are your enemy's fears? List them.

6. Do you see any similarities between your fears and those of your enemy? How do they relate to the fear of nonexistence?

7. You are a member of the Antifa group, and on a regular day while you are walking on the street doing some shopping, you see and recognize a member of the KKK. He is accidentally run over by a car. If you help him, you have no shadow; if you do not help him, you have a shadow. Explain.

8. How is violence, when used to defend an affective fuel, related to the fear of nonexistence? Explain.

CHAPTER 5

Polarization by Religious Fuel

Religion should unite all parts and cause all wars and disputes to vanish from the face of the earth, give birth to spirituality, and bring life and light to each heart. If religion becomes a cause of dislike, hatred, and division, it were better to be without it, and to withdraw from such a religion would be truly a religious act. For it is clear that the purpose of the remedy is to cure; but if remedy should only aggravate the complaint it had better be left alone. Any religion which is not a cause of love and unity is no religion.

—Abdu'l-Baha

Science has taken us to the moon; religion has flown us into buildings.

—Unknown

It is easy enough to be friendly to one's friends. But to befriend the one who regards himself as your enemy is the quintessence of true religion. The other is mere business.

—Mahatma Gandhi

People, I thought, wanted security. They couldn't bear the idea of death being a big black nothing, couldn't bear the thought of their loved ones not existing, and couldn't even imagine themselves not existing. I finally decided that people believe in an afterlife because they couldn't bear not to.

—John Green, *Looking for Alaska*

OF ALL THE affective fuels of ego integration, the most powerful of all is the religious fuel. The reason for this is that it is the only one that answers directly the fear of nonexistence, by guaranteeing existence after life with a series of preconditions. In order to understand the power this affective fuel has, one must understand that the driving force is precisely a profound fear of nonexistence. Otherwise religion would have no power. And of all the polarization mechanisms, perhaps the most powerful and most scary is the religious fuel.

Religion can be ego centered or self-less centered. When the religion is self-less centered, it tends to dissolve the sense of self and increase the sense of unity with other individuals and the world. When the religion is self-centered or ego centered, it tends to act as an affective fuel of ego integration and solidifies the sense of self to the exclusion of other individuals and even God himself. The main difference is that a self-less centered religion denies the self and the mechanisms of integration, but an ego-centered religion does, the opposite. For example, in some belief systems in the monasteries, the monks essentially renounce all the trappings of the world in an effort to deny the self and approach God. Other religious belief systems, however, emphasize the being or feeling special because one belongs to a particular belief system, and at the same time they emphasize feeling superior to or above other people. They may also emphasize rewards with pleasures in the afterlife. These belief systems essentially encyst the ego to the exclusion of other people and generate division, and this leads to violence.

Some characteristic differences between ego-centered and self-less centered religions are as follows.

People who are part of ego-centered religions

- place an emphasis on "self" salvation, a selfish approach
- dehumanize individuals with a different religious belief system
- feel superior for believing in a specific belief system
- discriminate against individuals with a different belief system
- believe that people are entitled to exert their will over that of someone who adheres to a different belief system—for example, taking over the possessions of another person, taking the life

of another person, enslaving another person, taking away the liberty of another individual

- expect to receive the affective fuels of ego integration that they don't have in this present life in the afterlife—for example, expect sexual pleasures, honors or material possessions, or adulation; observe that the emphasis is on maintaining the sense of ego integration and ego aggrandizement
- believe that one can be judgmental about another individual and even serve as executioner. In essence, the person is assuming God's role of judging an individual. (This can be considered blasphemy in some belief systems.)
- assume they know God's will and impose that belief on others

On the other hand, followers of selfless-centered religions

- realize that salvation is not obtained by one's individual actions, but rather by profound compassion of the divinity
- are more concerned about other people's salvation rather than their own
- submit themselves to others and for their benefit
- realize that one is nothing
- humanize strangers and even enemies to the point of loving them
- have no desire for affective fuels of ego integration but desire union with the divinity
- make personal sacrifices for others
- have respect for life
- have a capacity for forgiveness

Polarization by religious fuel takes three forms:

- hindering of assimilation to the wider society
- radicalization
- discrimination

Polarization by the hindering of assimilation can take place when the religious fuel of ego integration blocks assimilation by making individuals feel that they will be condemned if they accept the values and notions of the host culture. This concept is extremely powerful since it is based on the fear of nonexistence and it addresses fundamentally the individual sense of existence. If the religious belief system teaches that assimilation or acceptance of democracy is prohibited or will lead to condemnation, individual will likely block attempts at assimilation.

The mechanism of radicalization is clearly understood if one understands that the religious fuel promises existence after death with all the promises of the other affective fuels of ego integration—sexual pleasures (emotional-sexual fuel), honors and recognition (social fuel), treasures and riches (material fuel), knowledge (intellectual fuel), and being loved by God (religious fuel)—that one has in this reality and in the afterlife, with the precondition of an act of violence for this to be obtained.

Again, the driving force behind the radicalization process is a profound fear of nonexistence which is answered by a religious belief system that promises existence after death with the precondition of an act of violence to achieve paradise. Without the fear of nonexistence, this mechanism would have no power.

Observe that religion promises the affective fuels of ego integration in the afterlife that individuals may or may not have in this life. The most powerful affective fuel of ego integration is precisely the religious fuel because it is the only one that directly addresses the fear of nonexistence of the individual.

Examples of the above can be seen in the fact that, in 2017, members of a terrorist group began giving their fighters passports to heaven. This constitutes manipulation of the fear of nonexistence to induce the fighters to fight to their death without fear. Likewise, another religious teacher began preaching that paradise was like a sexual orgy (emotional-sexual fuel). In fact, he was promising one of the affective fuels of ego integration in the afterlife, in essence solidifying the sense of self.

The problem with all of this is that the concept of God or paradise is made submissive or tied down to the enhancement of the self, rather than the union with the absolute or what one construes to be God. The main trust of paradise then becomes a mechanism of ego integration or satisfaction of the sense of self, rather than the concept of union in which the individual achieves totality.

Polarization by discrimination takes place when individuals are taught that they will be less if they identify with a subgroup of individuals that they consider below them either intellectually or from the standpoint of a religious belief system. Again, the driving force is a profound fear of nonexistence. As described in a prior chapter on the mechanism of prejudice, the identification process is blocked due to the fear of becoming less and feeling more threatened by nonexistence. By feeling superior to the inferior group being discriminated against, the individuals have a false sense of superiority that shields them from the primary fear of nonexistence. This feeling of superiority leads to an ego expansion, which makes the sense of self feel more secure against nonexistence. Again, the driving force is this primary fear.

As an example of this, according to Kent Karlsson, rector at Tjarnaangs Swedish school, another religious school in Borlänge, Sweden, began teaching their children that they were superior, should only respect other individuals with the same religious belief systems, and refuse to listen to "white people," generating prejudice and racism against individuals who do not share their belief system. This apparently was being taught to children from six to thirteen years old. Correctly, he pointed out that this practice created more exclusion in already segregated areas. The education is being given at the level of the protoego, or early in the formation of the ego. Once it is interjected as part of the ego structure, it acts like a filter for other concepts that are interjected into the sense of self. It becomes very difficult then to later overcome the learned prejudice and racism. Eventually, this leads to division, conflicts, and even civil war. The reason the children are taught that they're superior is to counter the fear of nonexistence. By believing themselves superior, this reaffirms the sense of self against this primary fear. The sad part is that the teachers who are teaching this are ignorant and blind to their own fear and do not have an iota of introspection.

Religion can contribute to the formation of society, or it can lead to the dissolution of it. When religion works as a unitive force, it allows for the cohesion of society and facilitates the development of society and culture as a whole. When religion works as a dividing force, it has the opposite effect, actually working against the development of society. Many examples of this are found in Middle Eastern countries, where institutionalized discrimination against religious minorities on the basis of religion is the norm. Many of these countries suffer from significant social strife, terrorism, and internal division.

Although the main source of the social strife and division is a religious belief system that allows for discrimination and permits violence, no effort is made to have a frank discussion on it precisely because of the fear of condemnation triggered by the fear of nonexistence. Instead, the reason for this social strife is ascribed to other causes without really observing the actual mechanism.

Manipulation of the fear of nonexistence to promote violence through religious teachings, utilizing the religious fuel to counter the fear, also happens commonly. Many of these so-called religious teachers are blind themselves to their own motivations and their own fears and, by their teachings, make others twice as blind as they are. Many see sin in a woman's wearing a miniskirt but see no sin in the killing or taking of innocent life in the name of their religion. They justify this as being pleasing to their deity and believe it will win them a place in their concept of heaven. If we conceptualize a deity so vast and powerful that it is able to create the whole universe, the belief that any of our actions would change its will or opinion of us is wishful thinking. That would be tantamount to an ant's changing our opinion by doing a song and dance. The idea that our actions can save us is in reality a profound act of pride in the face of the creator. If God exists and we are saved, it is because of a profound act of compassion on his part, not because of any of our actions.

The only solution for this profound division in terms of religious fuel is twofold.

- Frank and open discussion is necessary in order to understand the mechanisms in terms of the fear of nonexistence.
- The individuals who are manipulating this fuel to promote violence and division have to be stopped and segregated from society so they cannot continue to spill their poison. Some would make an argument that this is illegal or restricting one's

freedom, citing free speech. (Recently, in Denmark a religious teacher was charged under the law for calling for the annihilation of a minority group.) However, because of the power of this fuel, allowing individuals to continue to radicalize others by manipulating their fear of nonexistence will result in more acts of violence in society. A careful line has to be drawn here to avoid the extreme of an Antifa movement, which prevents people who disagree with them from expressing their views even if their views are nonviolent and just disagreeable. Only when the views call for active violence and harming of others or overt denigration or discrimination of a particular group should action be taken, and then it should be taken in a nonviolent way under the confines of the law. Reeducation of these individuals, if possible, through the mechanism of introspection should be attempted, but under no circumstances should they be allowed to harm others or should they themselves be harmed. Several examples can be found in some Middle Eastern countries, where in some villages religious leaders fan violence against minorities and even advocate for the killing and destruction of their homes because of presumed or perceived offenses against their belief systems. The governments in these countries very frequently abdicate their responsibility to hold these religious leaders accountable because they share the same religious belief system. They cannot claim to be democratic countries with equal values for all as long as they continue in this course of action. These governments should be taken to the International Criminal Court and be held responsible for abdicating their responsibilities toward minorities. Separation of church and the state should be mandatory, and theocracies should not be allowed by the United Nations since they will invariably violate the rights of minorities with different religious beliefs systems.

Individual susceptibility to radicalization is based on several conditions.

- substitution of the religious affective fuel promoting violence by one promoting unity

- negation or weakening of the religious fuel advocating violence
- introspection to understand the mechanism
- formation of the protoego and its filters by the social and religious fuel at an early age, which may allow for discrimination and violence
- absence of other integrative fuels, which makes individuals more susceptible to manipulation by the religious fuel
- peer pressure in the form of social fuel, which allows for rejection of individuals if they do not conform to violence and radicalization
- lack of education, which prevents the acquisition of other affective fuels (this is closely related to the second item)
- a precipitating event, such as a rejection or traumatic event that may cause an acute ego contraction, which is painful and will make the individual fall back on the religious fuel as a mechanism of ego integration

A precipitating event may trigger a desire to lash out at individuals or society, where the perceived rejection took place. If the protoego has elements of the social and religious fuel that allow for violence, then individuals would use this as a mechanism to lash out defensively at what they perceive as an attack on their selves. If the individuals identify themselves with a group of people sharing a similar religious belief, an attack on this group of people would be perceived as an attack on the self. This is secondary to the identification mechanism, which acts as a mechanism of evolution by allowing the grouping of individuals according to a common belief system to preserve the species. This mechanism of grouping allows for the defense of the species against an outside threat and is also commonly seen in wild animals. From the evolutionary point of view, it may have been genetic at the beginning, but now it is progressing toward a mechanism dependent on the sense of self. It should be mentioned that a primitive self is beginning to be identified in some species. For example, mourning has been identified in elephants, as well as in some primates. This suggests a primitive sense of self. So the sense of self might not be exclusive to the human race.

In October 2017 in New York, a terrorist drove a truck onto a bicycle path to kill several civilians. When we look at the background of this individual (based on information obtained from the Internet and media outlets), several factors begin to appear, as mentioned above.

- The individual is from a foreign country and speaks a different language. His country of origin lacks an adequate education system and has a high unemployment rate, which makes integration difficult.
- The individual lacks an adequate education (intellectual fuel), which makes the acquisition of affective fuels of ego integration difficult.
- The individual feels relegated to an inferior position (social fuel) in the new society because of his lack of education and skills in a highly technological society.
- The individual has little or no significant economic acquisitive power, also negating him material fuel.
- The individual integrates himself on the religious affective fuel of his childhood, which tells him that he's superior because of his belief system and which also has tenets that promote violence.
- The individual identifies himself with the religious belief system of a terrorist group in the Middle East, which is under attack by several countries for its cruelty and its wanton killing. By identifying himself with that particular religious belief system, the person himself feels attacked, especially living in the society that is attacking the other terrorist group.
- The individual's partner, however, comes from a culture where she is treated as a second-class citizen, and therefore he doesn't base his sense of integration on the affective and emotional-sexual fuel since he considers his partner to be inferior to him. Identifying himself with what he considers to be an inferior person would lead to an ego contraction and increase his sense of threat by nonexistence. This is equivalent to the mechanism of prejudice described earlier.

Analyzing the above, we realize why this individual is prone to radicalization. He lacks all the affective fuels of integration to be able to feel safe against the fear of nonexistence in the newly acquired society and tends to integrate himself solely on the religious belief system that accepts violence as a religious tenet. This integration mechanism makes him identify with the individuals under attack by the coalition of countries, and he develops aggressivity because he himself is threatened in his integrity mechanism. This aggressivity eventually boils over into a violent act in an attempt to get back at the individuals he feels are threatening his mechanism of integration. The driving force behind it is a profound fear of nonexistence with the lack of a balance integration system in terms of affective fuels and integration solely on a specific affective fuel, which allows for violence.

So-called deradicalization programs that are being used to try to change the behavior of the radicalized individuals often fail in their purpose. The reason for this is that they fail to see the driving force behind the radicalization of the individual, which is a profound fear of nonexistence alleviated by a religious belief system. The protoego is formed at a very early stage by the religious and social fuels acquired from society and parental guidance. Once the religious and social fuels integrate the protoego, they serve as filters for any other affective fuels of ego integration coming into the self. The radicalization mechanism takes place at the level of the protoego, and therefore new fuels that would contribute to deradicalization will be filtered out and prevent changing the individual's frame of mind.

The only way the individual can be deradicalized is by changing these fuels at the level of the protoego. This is a painful process since the individual will feel that he is becoming less and therefore will feel more threatened by the fear of nonexistence. It is the equivalent of brainwashing, in the old parlance. A similar process takes place in the so-called conversion therapy of homosexual behavior. This process, largely abandoned by many therapists, is very painful to the sense of self, and when it is devoid of alternative fuels of ego integration, it can lead to the individual's becoming asexual. The reason many of these processes failed was precisely because they did not recognize the need for a substitution of the affective emotional-sexual fuel of ego integration by another who would allow the individual to feel complete and independent of the need for affection of the emotional-sexual fuel.

This is the equivalent of having an individual breathing underneath the water through a small tube and wanting to take that tube away without giving him another source of air. The individual will resist the change.

Some solutions that would work include the following:

- Recognize the effect of the social and religious fuels in forming the protoego and their effect as filters in other integrative fuels.
- Weaken the affective social and religious fuels and their parameters so that new fuels can be integrated into the protoego.
- Substitute the religious affective fuel, which promotes violence by a different religious affective fuel that promotes unity. Christianity would be a good substitution in view of its emphasis on unity rather than division. Buddhism would be another good choice, as well as Judaism and a moderate form of Islam. Encouragement to substitute the fuel can be given in the form of little privileges, like food and material goods that the individual can obtain by accepting the new fuel—the equivalent of a behavior-reward system.
- Add other affective fuels of ego integration, such as education, technology training, vocational training, and social and emotional-sexual fuel, so that the individual is not exclusively integrated on the religious fuel. The addition of different affective fuels weakens the dependence on a singular fuel of ego integration and allows for a transition to a different set of values.
- Isolate the individual from his original peer system, which may reinforce the original fuel, and placing the individual in a different support system that encourages the adoption of a new religious fuel. Many cases of religious radicalization can be traced back to the prison system, where a teacher converts a previously unradicalized individual by taking advantage of
  - o the individual's sense of isolation and rejection by society,
  - o promises of the affective fuels he lacks in the afterlife, and
  - o making him feel special or superior by believing in an specific religious belief system. Since the belief involves no physical or intellectual effort and is easily obtained, the individual falls for it.

- Make the individual feel more secure, appreciated, supported, and respected when he adopts a new religious belief system. This will reinforce the self against nonexistence and facilitate the transition.
- Although so far the emphasis has been on weakening and substituting a religious belief system, in selected individuals who show a high degree of intelligence, introspection can be attempted in order for them to understand the mechanism of affective fuels.
- Leaders within the community can be chosen who have already achieved a transition to a different belief system to help those who are in the process.
- Understand that the driving force behind the radicalization process is a profound fear of nonexistence, and any substitution of affective fuels has to eventually address this fear directly.
- Understand the difference between ego-centered religions and selfless-centered religions.

There is a lot of emphasis in our society on avoiding being selfish or egotistical. However, we live in a conflicted society, where on one hand we are advised not to be selfish, and on the other hand, we are encouraged to be egotistical. We may go to church or the temple and hear a sermon about being unselfish. But then we leave the church and are bombarded by the emphasis of being more, of having more power or more adulation. We encounter a shower of advertisements about the latest fashions, the best car, the best housing, the best education, and so on. The emphasis is on acquiring more without understanding why.

A long as we have a sense of self, there will be an element of selfishness. One cannot separate the sense of self from selfishness. We are all selfish or egotistical to some degree. At which point this level of selfishness becomes unacceptable to society is a relative value and depends on societal norms. We are always admonished to be more altruistic and less selfish, but the main mechanism of selfishness is not understood. That is why it becomes so difficult to be unselfish. Selfishness has its basis in the fear of nonexistence, against which the sense of self integrates itself by utilizing the different affective fuels. As explained in the section on social fuel regarding harassment, as the sense of self decreases either by understanding or discipline (for example, in a monastery), it becomes easier for the individual to become less selfish since there is less of a sense of self to require affective fuels. This process of becoming less selfish or more selfish is equivalent to being on top of a mountain and choosing one path to go down or the other. Whichever path one chooses will accelerate as one embarks on that path. If one chooses to be unselfish and accepts the discipline required to do it, then there is less need for affective fuels and the process of ego loss accelerates as the self begins to decrease. There is less of a sense of self to be threatened by nonexistence, and the process of letting go accelerates. If, on the other hand, one chooses to be selfish and materialistic, as the sense of self solidifies, it feels more threatened by nonexistence and requires more affective fuels, which accelerate the mechanism of egoism. There is not a stable platform or status quo. The mechanism is unstable by its nature. The process of ego loss or ego acquisition will accelerate depending on which path one takes.

One concept that we need to explore is that of union. If we look at different religious belief systems, we would almost invariably find reference to the concept of union. For example, the Buddhist tradition addresses the concept of enlightenment, *satori*. *Kensho* is one in which the individual is able to dissolve the sense of self and grasp the unity between things. Something similar happens in the Christian tradition with the concept of communion, or "common union," as well as in the Hindu tradition with the concept of nirvana, which is very similar to the other two concepts. Why this emphasis on the sense of union? If we allow for the concept of a divinity, it would appear that with the development of a sense of self, there would be a separation from this divinity. The concept of original sin can be construed to be the development of a sense of self or ego. This by itself would lead to the loss of that unity if we conceive God to be in everything. With the onset of a concept of self, the idea of sin appears, as well as the idea of shame of one's nakedness. Prior to that, people coexisted with the rest of nature in what was called paradise without realizing their difference from the rest of nature. This loss of union makes the sense of self feel incomplete. At the same time, once people develop a sense of self or existence, the fear of nonexistence appears. It goes hand in hand with the sense of existence. If one exists, one can stop existing. The sense of separation and insecurity will haunt the sense of self until the death of the organism. It is as if we needed to be or feel part of that God to feel complete. The result is that individuals will attempt to try and find that union or completeness in imperfect things around them. For example, they may try to find it in friends and with their family; their countries (nationalism); or via sports teams, professional associations, or other groups that will give them an imperfect sense of union. Likewise, they will try to fight the fear of nonexistence by integrating themselves with different affective fuels as previously described. The existence of individuals will be governed by the need for integration by affective fuels and by the need for union with different groups. One can even argue that the sense of union gives individuals a sense of security by also providing them with social affective fuels.

The feeling that an individual has a purpose in life directed by the divinity is another concept worth investigating. (This will be discussed in depth later.) We tend to anthropomorphize the concept of God by attributing him human characteristics such as anger, affection, jealousy, and others. God probably transcends all of our human characteristics. The concept of feeling we have a purpose in life adheres to our need to feel that we are special in front of this divinity. This is a form of affection that constitutes an affective fuel of ego integration as it makes individuals feel safer against the fear of nonexistence by utilization of religious affective fuel. More likely than not, it is us who need to find that purpose in life in order to find or recognize God through it. Again, we see here the difference between ego-centered belief, which makes us feel we are special, and God-centered belief, in which we recognize our nothingness and our dependence on him.

This concept of having a purpose in life is used by some religious belief systems to justify and promote violence. By believing that it is their duty to further the belief in a deity by force or violence and killing, the individuals feel that they have a special purpose. In essence, as we explained above, they are catering to their own sense of self to feel special or loved by that deity. By believing in having a special purpose or meaning in life, individuals perceive that they have value. The sense of value means that the individuals' egos are worth preserving. Just as you would preserve something valuable, people feel that they are worth preserving because of this attributed value. This in itself is a selfish act. The fact that this is not recognized by the teachers of those religious belief systems points to their lack of spiritual depth. It is used to manipulate people to commit acts of violence by appealing to their need for affective fuels, making them feel special or wanted by their deity. Surely, a deity who has created the whole universe is more than capable to do his own killing if he really wants to. He does not need our help. As a matter of fact, if we accept that we are endowed by free will by that deity, which we possess and exercise on a daily basis, it would be a contradiction if that deity wanted to force us to believe in him. It would even be a bigger contradiction if that deity would favor the use of violence to force a belief system.

It is time to discuss the concept of unity, to which I alluded briefly. Assuming God exists and is a divine entity, it seems logical that the creation stems from him and is probably all a part of God. This suggests a deep union between this divine entity and the creation. If we look at the different religious belief systems—for example, Christianity, Buddhism, and Hinduism—we see an undercurrent of this concept of union in all of them. In all three, the negation of the self is the mechanism whereby one is able to achieve or reacquire this lost union. For example, in Buddhism, individuals are able to stop the sense of self through meditation and eventually come to what is described as satori or kensho, which is in itself an enlightenment. Likewise in Christianity there is the concept of sainthood, which is obtained by the negation of the self and complete submission to the will of God, which also implies a profound union with God. Hinduism has the concept of nirvana, which also implies a profound union of all things. So the concept of union appears to be intrinsic in all three of these religious belief systems.

If we analyze the Bible, as I explained in chapter 2, original sin can be construed as the taking of this self-consciousness. When Genesis refers to the tree of knowledge, we have to understand that knowledge is based on the ability to discriminate and stratify concepts in terms relative to oneself. For example, an animal, even though it may possess a primitive sense of self, is unable to stratify, segregate, and order a system. Human beings, with the acquisition of a sense of self, are able to stratify a system in terms that are relative to the sense of self. The justification takes place in terms of importance, effects, results, and other qualities. In essence, this stratification requires a sense of self to be performed. By eating from the tree of knowledge, individuals are essentially acquiring a consciousness that allows them to perform this task and become aware of sin as pertaining to sins that are or are not detrimental to their existence. The concept of eating pertains to the fact that a living organism has to acquire sustenance in order to exist. Once individuals have a self, they need to consume affective fuels of ego integration to maintain the integration of the sense of self. Thus, the act of eating an apple represents an allegorical description of the need of the self to start consuming affective fuels to maintain that integration. The consumption of affective fuels now triggers a necessity for them. This necessity in turn tends to categorize things as good or bad depending on whether they provide affective fuels. Thus, the concept of good and evil starts being defined by the acquisition or loss of affective fuels. The religious belief systems tend to modulate something good or bad in terms of affective fuels. It is in this concept of good and bad that one begins to see also the difference between ego centered religions and selfless centered religions. In ego centered religions, anything that deprives the sense of self from an affective fuel is considered bad, and anything that facilitates the acquisition of an affective fuel for the sense of self is considered good. In selfless centered religions, the opposite is true. Anything that negates an affective fuel to the sense of self and have to dissolution is considered good, and anything that facilitates the acquisition of an affective fuel and the further integration of the sense of self is considered bad. This acquisition of self-existence or self-knowledge comes with the price of separation from this absolute. One can construe the expulsion from paradise, described in the Bible as the separation that takes place from the absolute when the sense of self comes into existence—in other words, the loss of innocence. For example, a baby may walk naked into a room full of people and would more likely than not cause people to smile and try to hug and cuddle him or her. If an adult were to do the same, the reaction will be totally the opposite; the person would be called a pervert, and the police may be called. What is the difference? The difference is that we recognize the innocence of a child, and this innocence is precisely because the child has no concept of right or wrong because of this union that he has with the absolute—"no self." We are able to recognize this innocence (union) and rejoice in its existence. With adults, however, we also recognize that there's a loss of innocence and an ulterior motive. In order to have an ulterior motive, there needs to be a self that is able to prioritize and stratify goals. The baby has no ego yet, but the adult does.

We can see, then, that the separation takes place from this absolute when the sense of self is acquired. The separation is painful because we go from being one in innocence with the absolute to feeling isolated, segregated, and fractionated. Fear sets in due to the presence of nonexistence, and pain makes its entrance into the world. As I explained before, we tend to try to satisfy this need for union in the imperfect things around us—for example, nationalism, professional societies, family, friends, and so on. All these attempts are imperfect by their own nature and only satisfy the need for union on a temporary basis. Thus, as I explained in chapter 2, the loss of a loved one can cause profound pain due to the loss of this imperfect union, which is an attempt to re-create that perfect union we had before the taking of consciousness. It is only when we accept the self as a learned behavior and understand that we need to transcend it and approach this union again that we can find peace. The sense of peace comes from the sensation of at last feeling complete again in the union with the absolute. This is probably a very profound reason why people with a lot of psychological pain sometimes opt for suicide as a mechanism of rejoining this absolute. The paradox is that although we are afraid of nonexistence, it is only when we embrace the loss of self (i.e., self-nothingness) that we embrace this absolute and feel complete again.

Sometimes, God allows his absence to be felt between us so that we may learn to find him not at the expense of others but in each other by experiencing our mutual union.

The Sense of Meaning or Significance of Religious Fuel

Very often, individuals will try to develop a sense of meaning in their lives or create significance with their lives. For example, a mother who loses a child tragically to a car accident may want to make the death of that child significant for others and for herself, and she may also try to find significance or meaning in her personal life by embarking on a mission to protect others from accidents or tragedies like the one her daughter experienced. As commendable as this is, and I would probably do the same, when we look at it objectively, what the mother is trying to do is create a sense of permanence from the fear of death. This obeys the desire of the sense of self to find permanence itself, not only for the individual but also for others the individual regards as part of his or her affective fuels of integration. This is not to minimize the sense of pain or sadness that the individual who suffers the loss incurs. Having been through it myself three times in my life, I can attest to the profound sorrow and psychological pain that this can create. Nevertheless, this desire for meaning or significance in one's life is closely associated to the desire for permanence from part of the self. When this desire for significance or meaning in life is associated with religious belief systems and people believe that their lives have meaning or significance when they die for their religious belief systems, this can be a source of polarization. Several concepts need to be understood.

- The desire for meaning or significance is a desire to become important and thus worth preserving by what the individuals consider to be a deity that would grant them this for the sacrifice they have made.
- This desire to have meaning or significance is a desire of permanence by the sense of self, which serves to counteract the fear of nonexistence.
- At the very bottom of this desire is a selfish desire for existence of the sense of self.
- When the desire for meaning or significance is coupled to a religious belief system that demands the performance of a violent act in order to achieve it, the person will become radicalized.

We can see, then, that this desire for meaning or significance is just another selfish attempt by the sense of self to obtain permanence against the fear of nonexistence. The paradox is that as long as one desires to obtain this permanence, one is still orbiting around the fear of nonexistence. This fear would reappear after each attempt by the sense of self to find significance or meaning in life. It is only when one surrenders to service to others that the focus shifts from the desire of the self for permanence to the desire to help others at the expense of oneself. When this shift in focus takes place, the "flashlight" shifts from focusing on the sense of self to focusing on orders. The sense of self stops being operational, there is no more self-attention, and the psychological pain of the fear of nonexistence disappears.

An example of the above can be found in the life of Mother Teresa of Calcutta. She was not trying to find meaning to her life by helping others, but by surrendering to others and loving others, she shifted her attention from her own self toward other people. By that process, without looking for a sense of meaning or significance in her life, she eventually found her true meaning and significance in surrendering to others. This is the paradox. As long as we try to find significance or meaning, it evades us. It is only when we surrender to others without regard to the self that this meaning or significance is found. At the risk of becoming too spiritual, I suspect strongly that in this process of surrendering to others we begin to discover a profound realization of the unity we have with one another. When we forget about the sense of self, somehow, that appears to be a glimpse or a glimmer of the sense of unity, which becomes deeper as we exercise this surrendering to others more. The problem is that in this unity there is not a self to enjoy the sense of unity. During the active moment of unity, there is no self-consciousness. It is only when the self reattaches itself that we can look at it backward and realize what we experienced. In total union there is no self; in total self, there is no union.

The Concept of Sacrifice and Religious Polarization

The concept of sacrifice has to be understood from two perspectives. In the Abrahamic religions, Abraham is asked to sacrifice his son Isaac to God. At face value, it would appear that he was only sacrificing a son. But from the perspective of affective fuels, the sacrifice has five different levels. From the social fuel perspective, the sacrifice of a son implies the loss of social affective fuel, company, associations, and camaraderie. From the religious affective fuel perspective, he is going against a moral imperative not to kill. This in turn would make him guilty of taking a life. From the intellectual fuel perspective, the loss of a son implies the loss of the potential to pass on knowledge and interact with another individual to foment one's own growth. From the material fuel perspective, the loss of a son would adversely impact the ability to plow the fields and acquire material fuel since the children were often helpers in cultivating the fields and herding the cattle. Finally, from the perspective of emotional-sexual fuel, the loss of a child would also be the loss of affection for the parents.

We can see that the command to sacrifice a child impacts all the affective fuels at that time and era. The net result is a profound ego contraction which makes the sense of self totally and completely vulnerable to the experience of God. The active and complete act of total trusting and being willing to sacrifice one's will is the negation of one's will, and thus the complete abandonment of one to the mercy of God. Notice that what God requires from Abraham is the complete and total negation of the self in the form of affective fuels and the total submission of his will to God's will.

So let's understand this from two different perspectives. If the sacrifice is at the expense of one's own ego, it is selfless in nature and opens one up to the experience of the divinity. It is interesting to note that even when God asked Abraham to sacrifice his child, he never allowed him to proceed with it. It was the intention that God was pursuing, not the actual taking of a life. This also points out the deep respect God has for life. On the other hand, when the sacrifice is performed with expectation of a reward, the intention is not a surrendering of the self but the expectation of an increase in self by the reward attained. This is in itself a selfish desire devoid of any altruistic value (desire of acquisition).

With this, we can understand that the radicals, who sacrificed themselves by blowing themselves up along with other people with expectation of a reward, are motivated by a selfish desire and not by a true spirit of selfless sacrifice. In addition by taking innocent lives in their pursuit of a reward they are assuming God's role and violating God's own respect for life.

While still in the subject of sacrifice, one can explore the concept of sacrifice in the figure of Christ. This concept of Christ's sacrifice has to be looked at in perspective to the concept of sin since it is through his sacrifice that in the Christians' Abrahamic law and Moses's law the individuals are washed of their sins. Let us explore the concept of sin first according to Romans 7. An individual commits a sin when he or she acts against the law. The law was assumed to be the in the forms of the Ten Commandments. One can theorize that the initial tenets of the law were intended to prevent social conflict between individuals and facilitate social cohesion at a time of persecution and environmental harshness in the Jewish people. These laws, whether divinely inspired or not (I believe they were), went against the desire of the self to obtain affective fuels of ego integration.

For example, the first commandment relates to the worship of God above anything else. This pertains to the negation of the self and all the other affective fuels. The second commandment addresses worshiping material things ("graven images"), social respect, fame, and so on as our god. The third commandment warns against taking the name of the God in vain, meaning we should not use his name for our personal gain. Again, this comes down to the negation of the self.

The fourth commandment refers to sanctifying one certain day. This relates to the profound recognition of a deity and perhaps encourages us to use that day for reflection rather than for the acquisition of affective fuels. The fifth commandment refers to honoring the mother and the father. Here we see the command to actually love of our parents. We could interpret this as saying we should go against the desire of the sense of self to become independent of the affection of our parents as a mechanism of ego integration. Remember that the mother and father originally give their children the five affective fuels of integration in the form of social, religious, material, intellectual, and emotional fuels. Sometimes during adolescence, children will try to become independent of their parents and will look for these fuels outside the family. They realize the dependence they have on these fuels and subconsciously have a fear of losing them. Therefore, they begin to go against the parents in an attempt to reaffirm their identity by obtaining affective fuels outside the family environment. The affective fuels they try to obtain are fuels that they can control and that do not depend on the family. This leads to the very common adolescent rebellion against the parents. By commanding respect for the parents, in a way, the commandment is blocking up the desire to seek these affective fuels and to moderate the integration process of the self.

The other five commandments essentially address killing, committing adultery, stealing, bearing false witness, and coveting. All these commandments pertain to the acquisition of social, material, intellectual, or emotional-sexual fuels in order to integrate the sense of self.

One can see that the commandments are essentially blocking or moderating the acquisition of affective fuels at the expense of other individuals to prevent conflict, but more importantly to maintain a sense of humility (understand this as facilitating an ego contraction) so as to bring us closer to this absolute.

In Romans 7, Paul reflects on the fact that the law makes him aware that the desire of the sense of self in obtaining these affective fuels make him sin. He also goes on to reflect on the fact that the passions of the mind (the self) draw him away from God and into sin. So again we see the concept that the acquisition of affective fuels by solidifying the sense of self makes us stray further away from this absolute or God. Paul goes on to reflect on this trouble between the passions of the body and the desire of the mind from the spirit. He goes on to explain how, through Christ, one is liberated from the law that had caused him to die to sin. So how does Christ liberate us from the law? First, one must understand that the law in itself is not bad. It is not the intention of the law to make us die to sin but to make us aware of where sin is located. Once individuals become aware of this through the law, the conflict between the desire of the self to acquire an affective fuel of ego integration and the law begins. This is then a struggle that when the people falter, they die to sin through the law. The figure of Christ is transcendent then in that it brings with it hope.

If we look at the definition of *faith*, we see that a large component of that definition is hope and the other component is trust. The component of hope, which is in essence a desire of acquisition, pertains not to acquisition of the affective fuels but to the acquisition of unity with the absolute, or God. The paradox is that in this unity, the sense of self essentially disappears. The passions begin with the self and eventually, when the self loses itself in God, it is complete; there's no need to acquire to feel complete, and it is at peace. Thus it is with faith in Christ, the first level of faith, which is where hope shifts the desire of the self from the desire to acquire affective fuels to the desire to obtain unity with God. This is why Paul states that the individual loses the desire to sin, because the perspective changes. The second aspect of faith is trust. Trust is the relinquishing of one's own will to the will of another—in this, case God. It is the will of the individual who serves his need to obtain affective fuels. It is through the will that the individual seeks out the different affective fuels to try and maintain himself integrated against this primal fear of nonexistence. By surrendering his will in the act of trusting God, the individual gives up the mechanism of obtaining the affective fuels. First he loses the desire to obtain the affective fuel by the hope of union with God. And second, he gives up the mechanism to obtain this affective fuel by giving up his will by trusting God. The end result is a progressive ego contraction and the dissolution of the self, which leads one closer to that, God or absolute. Those are the two aspects of faith—hope and trust—and they manifest themselves as an antidote to the affective fuels of ego integration.

With this background, we can begin to explore the sacrifice of Christ more in depth. First of all we have an individual who, according to the Scriptures, has a dual nature, human and divine. By the divine's becoming human, it unites with humanity. It is God who, aware of the need of humanity to join him, takes the first step into the incarnation as a human being, becoming one with us. This reminds me of a story of a farmer who had a gaggle of geese and there was a storm coming. As long as he tried to herd them into a shelter, they would just scatter away and stay outside. Then he realized that all the geese would follow a leader. So he grabbed the leader, put him into the shelter, and watched all the geese follow him. He realized that it took one of their own for them to follow. By the same token, Christ by becoming human gives us something tangible to follow, not an abstract idea or concept. By becoming human, he now has a universal self or ego, which encompasses each and every single one of us. By sacrificing himself back to the father, he sacrifices that universal self or ego back to the absolute. Several things take place with the sacrifice.

First is the dissolution of his own self. By dissolving his self and giving up his life, he experienced a profound ego contraction since he was in essence giving up all the affective fuels that his human nature had. But at the same time, since he has embraced and joined all of us, he pulled us into that sacrifice through his love, understanding that true love is the profound realization of one's true nature in another human being. In this case the profound realization of Christ is that he was one with all of us through his human nature. Second, by telling God or asking him why he had forsaken him, Christ expressed the fear of nonexistence. For many of the Jewish tribes, the absence of God's love meant the dissolution of the soul, or nonexistence. The concept of a permanent soul was a Greek concept, not Jewish. Third, by sacrificing himself to the father, he made us the father's cause, the same way that a mother loses a child in a drunk driving accident and makes the child's death her call to work against drunk driving. Fourth, by experiencing pain and suffering, he showed that he knows the fear of death that we would all go through at one point in our lives. And fifth, through the Virgin Mary, he makes us aware that the divinity or the absolute also knows the most profound pain that one can have, which is the loss of a child.

By having faith in him, we fulfill two conditions. The first condition is that we shift from the desire to sin to the desire for unity through hope, and the second condition is that we relinquish the mechanism of affective fuels acquisition by relinquishing our will to our trust in him. This leads to a profound ego contraction and the release of the human self into the realm of the spirit, which does not desire to sin, because the only thing it wishes for is unity with God.

Christianity: The Weakest Link or the Proverbial Canary in the Cave?

Out of all the religious belief systems, there's one that warrants close examination and analysis because of what seems to be a contradictory message for existence. If we look at other religious systems, we'll notice an emphasis on expanding the religious belief systems by force, discrimination, segregation, revenge, and other forceful methods. Christianity, on the other hand, sends an opposite message, which at first glance makes it appear to be weak. For example, the concept of "loving your enemy" appears several times in the Bible, an idea that seems counterintuitive. Loving someone who wants to kill you or destroy you is not very conducive to existence. It would make more sense to destroy your enemy so that you can survive and continue to exist. Likewise, the concept of giving forgiveness over taking revenge also seems counterproductive. By obtaining revenge, we could instill fear in someone who hurt us and perhaps prevent further acts against us. Another concept that goes against humans' self-interest is that of being selfless and helping others. Why would we do this? And is it illogical? A deeper analysis, however, reveals that this behavior actually is conducive to the survival of not only the individual but also that of society. An enemy is someone who threatens our affective fuel and our sense of survival. When people begin to love an enemy, two things happen: first, they stop being a threat to the enemy's affective fuels, and second, the love that they profess may lead them to actually help the "enemy". They have transformed themselves from a threat in the enemy's eyes to people who want to help the enemy. This leads to a decrease in hostility and ensures the survival of both individuals at a deeper level. The act of loving your enemy implies that you recognize God's nature in your enemy also. In doing so, you cannot hurt your enemy any more than you could hurt God if you were to face him. Likewise, when you forgive, even though your sense of self does not experience unexpected expansion as it would with revenge, there is a sense of release from being bound to the concept of acquisition of an affective fuel (in this case, revenge). This allows individuals to focus their energy on other matters at hand and to function in society at a more normal level. In addition, if someone who has wronged another person feels forgiven, this might lead the individual to look at the other person in a different light and perhaps start a dialogue that will end the animosity. The offender, by not receiving retaliation against his action, is shaken from the you-versus-me concept, which may lead to a humanization of the individual he or she has wronged.

This concept of loving and forgiving your enemy actually tends to humanize people and start bringing about a sense of unity by allowing both individuals to recognize God in each other, the first step in humanizing another human being. It starts by recognizing that others are also dependent on affective fuels as you are and that you both have a common need. When interaction begins, then the sense of self begins to drop its barriers, and the recognition of God in each other begins.

So what appears to be a weakness in Christianity is actually its biggest strength. By breaching the divisions caused by affective fuels, Christianity is able to minimize conflict between individuals and allow for cooperation between them for a common good. This goes from the individual or micro scale to the population or macro scale. In doing so, it tends to stabilize society and allow for its growth and development technologically, socially, and spiritually. To assess the deep impact of this concept of forgiveness and loving your enemy, we need only to look at the Middle East and the European countries. We can see where the conflict is, what feeds the conflict, and where the people fleeing the conflict are taking refuge.

The figure of Christ is a controversial one and warrants close examination and analysis from the perspective of affective fuels. Here we have an individual who, from the beginning of his life, preached love, compassion, tolerance, and union. From the perspective of social fuel, he was not looking for adoration, respect, or admiration. In terms of religious fuel, he preached tolerance, compassion, and unity and submitted his will to that of God. As for material fuel, he did not look for riches, possessions, or status, and regarding intellectual fuel, he did not boast about his knowledge and preached humility. In terms of emotional-sexual fuel, he was celibate, and rather than look for affection to be given to him, he gave affection. We can even question whether he had a sense of self or not. This is an individual who declined all the affective fuels and whose main teaching was about the concept of unity, love, if we can define *love* as the profound realization of your own true self in another person. His message throughout his life, culminating in the Last Supper with the institution of "communion" (common union), was always one of union. It is as if he profoundly realized the union that permeates all of creation. One thing that has impressed me is that even when he was being crucified and tortured, his message of forgiveness and compassion did not waver. It takes a remarkable human being (if he was human at all) to maintain this solid conviction of compassion and unity throughout life, without wavering even when under extreme duress and distress. He did not seem to be affected by the affective fuels. He expressed no need for them. He existed as a manifestation of unity throughout his life. If one understand that for the Jewish people, the soul was not permanent and only existed as long as God provided his love for it, then the concept of resurrection takes on a new meaning in this perspective. Here is an individual claiming to be the son of God who is devoid of any need for affective fuels and preaching unity all the time, even at the time of his death. Then, according to the biblical Scriptures and many other historical texts, he is resurrected after three days. The concept of resurrection is a direct attack on the fear of nonexistence. It has meaning only if we can understand that it is directed against the fear of nonexistence that we all have. In order to clarify this concept, we need to understand how Christ actually provides peace and serenity to those in need. The sense of self tries to integrate itself against the fear of nonexistence by the affective fuels, as explained in prior chapters. Once we take consciousness, there is a sense of incompleteness that permeates our whole lives. We try to compensate for the sense of incompleteness by the consumption of affective fuels, feeling only temporary relief. The acquisition of an affective fuel alleviates the fear of nonexistence for a time, but then it reappears, only to drive us to try to obtain another affective fuel. This is a vicious circle, which repeats itself over and over again. By dying for all of us on the cross, Christ embraced that fear for all of us and united with us in the fear of nonexistence. By resurrecting, he reaffirmed the love of God for all of us and possibly the preservation of our relative consciousness. With his mantle, he covers all of us, and because God loves his son and we are all covered by his mantle, in turn we are all preserved through him. We experience a sense of peace when we unite with Christ because in that union, for the first time, we feel complete again. When we feel fully complete, the desire to acquire affective fuel disappears. We revert to a state of serenity or peace, which is the natural state of human beings. If we understand that through the union with God, we feel totally complete and the desire for acquisitions of affective fuels disappears, then by corollary we can understand that if Christ was in union with God, he had no need for affective fuels, and then we understand *why* he had no need for them. He had no need for affective fuels because he has a union with God. He's complete in his totality, he has no desire for affective fuels or for ego integration, and he's driven by love streaming from the sense of unity that he realizes in everything. In order for him to have that union, he has to be part of God, or the Son of God himself, as he stated.

Questions:

1. Do you hold to any specific religious belief system? Why? Does it guarantee your existence after death?

2. Does your religious belief system make you feel superior or special compared to others? Why do you need to feel superior or special? Does this make you feel more secure? Against what?

3. How can you see God in your enemy? Is he or she human?

4. Imagine that you hold a religious belief system that tells you that you should kill those who don't believe like you. You travel as a tourist to another country, and when they find out your religious belief system, you're immediately arrested. They tell you that their religious belief system commands them to execute you because their God dislikes you. You try to explain to them that you follow the true God, only for them to tell you that *theirs* is the true God. How do you feel? Can you see how somebody that you dislike would feel?

5. How does advocating violence for your religious belief system make you feel? Do you feel special for defending your religious belief system? Why? Does it make you feel special to the deity that you believe in? Do you expect a reward for using violence against others? What does this reward consist of? Does it have to do with self-permanence?

6. How do you realize God in your enemy? Does he or she have the same fears you do? What fears do you share with him or her? How does he or she compensate for his or her fears, and how do you compensate for yours? Do you see any similarity?

7. Explain forgiveness.

8. You die and you go to heaven. You still have a sense of self, which means that you are bound by all the affective fuels. Do you think that God in all his power will be able to satisfy the affective fuels? Do the affective fuels have a limit? Would you still carry the fear of nonexistence into the afterlife? If so, how can God satisfy you completely if, after every ego integration, the same fear of nonexistence reappears? Can you explain how the concept of unity may actually give a solution to this paradox?

9. You die and you go to heaven. You are in front of the creator. Next to you is a sinner who also died. The creator tells you that you are saved and you will enter Paradise. He turns to the sinner and tells him he's condemned and will go to hell. The sinner is crying. In an act of compassion, you turn to the creator and you ask him to let the sinner go into paradise and you will go to hell in his place for eternity. What do you think God's reaction would be? Can you have more compassion than him?

CHAPTER 6

Polarization by Intellectual Fuel

I only know that I know nothing.

—Socrates

I wish I could make them understand that a good heart is riches enough, and that without it intellect is poverty.

—Mark Twain

Watch out for intellect, because it knows so much, it knows nothing and leaves you hanging upside down, mouthing knowledge as your heart falls out of your mouth.

—Anne Sexton

Wise men speak because they have something to say; fools because they have to say something.

—Plato

Some people think only intellect counts: knowing how to solve problems, knowing how to get by, knowing how to identify an advantage and seize it. But the functions of intellect are insufficient without courage, love, friendship, compassion, and empathy.

—Dean Koontz

POLARIZATION BY INTELLECTUAL fuel begins at an early age in society. The first indication of this is the segregation of young children by intellectual capacity. For example, in the United States, schools have several different programs in which children are segregated into different classes by intellectual ability (gifted programs). This polarization continues when people are accepted to high school and subsequently to a university. The acceptance into a famous or high-level university guarantees individuals, in most cases, adequate jobs that, in turn, translate into the acquisition of material fuels in the future by increasing the acquisitive power. Competition for acceptance into a well-known university can be seen in many countries. For example, in India recently on 2018 there was a scandal because apparently there was a lot of cheating during the university entrance exam by many students. The fact that this even made the newspapers highlights the level of importance that people give to the acquisition of intellectual material fuel.

The acquisition of intellectual fuel translates later in life to the ability to obtain material fuel and even emotional-sexual fuel. Whereas in ancient times, when the economy was a subsistence economy, physical fitness and perhaps size (material fuel) were advantages, in our modern society, which is highly technologically advanced, intellectual fuel appears to be the main mechanism to acquire the other affective fuels. The polarization that results has even coined words to describe it. For example, intellectuals are often called nerds, and athletes are called jocks. Each particular group begins to find their mechanisms of identity as individuals are drawn to people with the same interests.

The segregation of children into different levels of education in elementary and high school is an example of micropolarization. This process continues after college, and after individuals are able to find jobs and are stratified into a particular class, the process of macropolarization begins to take place, depending on their job status. For example, individuals who may not have been able to obtain a college education due to intellectual capacity, circumstances, or economic reasons may tend toward blue-collar work. On the other hand, individuals with a higher intellectual capacity who may come from affluent families or have a specific set of circumstances may drift into higher-paying jobs and corporate positions. In many countries, this difference is being dampened by helping people acquire scholarships, so that individuals with poor economic backgrounds can obtain an adequate education.

Blue-collar workers' development of unions to obtain benefits from corporations represents the end result of macropolarization by intellectual fuel. With the advent of technology, artificial intelligence, and robotics, many blue-collar workers are being displaced and either have to be retrained or are falling into poverty. We need to understand that we have a responsibility to all of society. Higher ability—in this case, intellect—carries higher responsibility. But this responsibility cannot be directed toward ourselves and our immediate families only; it has to be understood in terms of society as a whole. Our educational system is failing by providing a technological education without also providing the moral compass to guide individuals once that education is achieved. Instead of saying education is a mechanism to advance oneself and obtain other affective fuels of ego integration, education should be balanced so that individuals, through introspection and understanding of the self, realize that the gift of education carries with it a profound responsibility to help other, less fortunate individuals. The acquisition of material fuels, emotional-sexual fuels, and social fuels such as honors, recognition, and respect should be secondary to the realization that one has to help other people with the intellectual skills that have been acquired. There's nothing wrong with utilizing intellectual abilities to provide for our families and to provide shelter and food. The problem begins when the sense of self is allowed to run like an uncontrolled horse and continues to try to obtain more and more material fuels, more emotional-sexual fuel, and more honors, thinking that will bring security to the sense of self. The government cannot impose a moral conscience on anyone. The moral conscience to do good for people can only be acquired by individual people through the exercise of profound introspection and the realization of the profound unity that each individual has with other people around him or her and with nature.

By understanding how the sense of self integrates itself with different affective fuels, people can liberate themselves from the need to acquire them to feel secure against the fear of nonexistence. At this level, individuals begin to realize that they don't need to acquire things in the form of honors, material things, or emotional-sexual fuels to feel secure. It is solely with this deep understanding that people are able to free themselves from the mechanism of integration of the self and then assume responsibility not only for their own well-being but also for those around him.

So far we have discussed intellectual polarization by the mechanism of education. However, other forms of intellectual polarization do take place. Recently as reported on "foreign Policy.com" in China, people employed as thought monitors were incorporated into the universities to make sure that the students and faculty do not deviate from a specific ideology. The idea is that by making sure no ideas or thoughts different from those approved by the government reach people's minds, the ruling party can maintain or preserve its ideological preponderance. The problem with this approach is twofold.

- By stifling new ideas, they are essentially blunting the intellectual evolutionary process that is necessary for a society to develop. Ideas that may have been in vogue forty or sixty years ago may not apply to modern times, and new ideas might be necessary in order for society to continue its evolutionary process. The end result is a homogeneous, stale intellectual society that is poorly equipped to adapt to the changing social environment.
- The fallacy of believing that by controlling thought or monitoring thought the ruling party can prevent deviation from the main line of thinking points to a profound lack of understanding of the psychology of the human mind. As society evolves, new affective fuels of ego integration develop. The sense of self will necessarily look for these new affective fuels to maintain integration in the new society. By blocking access to them, the ruling party is essentially generating a pressure cooker in which individuals will try to look for new affective fuels of ego integration regardless of what the government tries to do. An example of this was Tiananmen Square.

Another example of how attempts to control people's way of life and minds fail is what happened with the demonstrations in Iran in 2011–2012 and then in 2017–2018. In these cases, we saw an attempt to establish a rigid ideology that controls not only what people think (intellectual fuel) but also how people dress and what they eat (material fuel), how they relate to God (religious fuel), and how they are allowed to interact with members of the opposite sex (emotional-sexual fuel, social fuel). This is an example of a theocracy with extensive influence on the religious aspects of people's lives as well as other aspects embedding itself in people's everyday living and impacting all the affective fuels. As in the case of China, the leaders' mistake is to try to exercise strict control over people who are able to exercise control over their own thoughts. What they again fail to realize is that once they block an affective fuel of ego integration, the human psyche will develop a new strategy to try to integrate itself. If they block all the mechanisms of ego integration, the end result is that the sense of self feels blocked in its attempt to integrate itself against the primal fear of nonexistence, and at that point, it will feel severely threatened. It will lash out with violence against what it perceives to be a form of government that prevents individuals from looking for new affective fuels of ego integration. If one of the affective fuels is controlled, the tendency for the sense of self is to look for a new mechanism or a strategy of ego integration, and although some social discontent might be present, individuals will tend to tolerate this psychological discomfort as long as they are able to integrate themselves in other fuels. For example, in Cuba, where there is a strong dictatorship and an attempt has been made to block all the mechanisms of ego integration, the citizens have looked for different strategies to cope with the limitations that they face in obtaining some affective fuels. Alcoholism is prevalent, and many professionals unable to achieve material fuel within their professions may turn to prostitution, such as is the case with "*jineteras*". Many of these "jineteras" are professionals in the medical or other fields but were unable to make a living in those professions to obtain material fuel, so they turned to prostitution with tourists as a way of acquiring them. One can always tell when a government is able to provide for the affective fuels of integration and allows the freedom to pursue them by observing from which country individuals desire to leave and to what countries they desire to go.

Five hundred or six hundred years ago, the affective fuels available for individuals to integrate their sense of self were limited. They may have been involved with agricultural, soldiering, and perhaps the pursuing of some limited intellectual activities. Five hundred years later, there's a proliferation of affective fuels from which people can choose one or the other to integrate the sense of self, such as medicine, astronomy, physics, mathematics, engineering, agricultural sciences, monastic life, flying airplanes, marine sciences, and so on. Likewise, social fuels also evolve. The relationships between people five hundred years ago with regard to marriage, cohabitation, dating, and family procreation are much different from the ones that we have now. The proliferation of new affective fuels and social pressures will drive people to look for new intellectual and social fuels to adapt to the new environment. Efforts to block the acquisition of new affective fuels of ego integration will fail precisely because the mind needs to acquire them in order to maintain the sense of integration.

The role of a government thus should not be to try and control the way people live their lives and what they think, even with respect to religion. It should be a facilitator for the individuals within the society to achieve their different mechanisms of ego integration, and it should interfere only to protect the lives and well-being of individual members of society when the acquisition of an affective fuel by a group begins to physically endanger or violate the rights of another individual. In addition, it should be the guarantor of equal rights for everyone, independent of their social, religious, material, intellectual, or sexual status. In other words, the government cannot be in the business of dictating to individuals what affective fuels they should pursue. It is only there to protect the rights of everyone equally, without distinction, and to facilitate the acquisition of affective fuels so that society can evolve spontaneously. I cannot emphasize enough the need for equal rights for everyone. The government cannot align itself with a specific ideology or religion since this will discriminate against a group with the opposite belief systems. This is the great failure of many countries in the Middle East and thus explains the violence, destruction, poverty, lack of education, and human suffering present in those countries. As an adjuvant to good governance, the government may attempt only through a humanistic education to promote a sense of unity between all members of society by helping them recognize their own humanity in others.

At this point we can begin to discuss the role of education in society. Many countries believe that educated individuals are highly educated in technology, mathematics, sciences, biology, and the like. These individuals are essentially intellects without direction. They may as well be called robots. Besides the technological and mathematical aspects of it, a true education leads people to not only think and analyze their relationship with the society in which they live, but more importantly helps them analyze the relationship with themselves. Only when people truly understand themselves can they begin understanding others. Only when people understand their motivations, needs, desires, and fears are they truly free from them and able to then start understanding others in the same way. Humanism is not a byproduct of a classical education. Humanism is the result of a profound understanding of our human nature so that we can extrapolate that understanding to others and realize our own humanity in them. A classical education, advocated by many top international colleges, is a waste of time and intellect, unless individuals learn to understand themselves in depth and face their own fears. Ignorance of our own fears is what makes us lash out against others when our affective fuels are threatened, and it is the primal fear that is the driving force behind it.

I remember a philosophical department from a not-to-be-mentioned university that, in a spite of all their philosophical and classical education, lacked the humanity to reach out to one of their own members who happened to think differently from them. The individual in question was ostracized to the point that all his affective fuels failed. The individual attempted to compensate in different ways through alcoholism, hoarding, and isolation, eventually ending up in a passive suicide. What did the classical and philosophical education serve the members of this department for? Where was their humanity? Where was their compassion? Aren't they supposed to be the vanguard, the light, so to speak, to teach us ethics and humanity? Toilet tissue is more useful than all their wasted years pursuing a classical or philosophical education.

When education becomes a mere exercise in intellectual achievement devoid of a sense of meaning or reason for this education and fails to increase our knowledge or perception of the unity between us and fails to increase our sense of compassion for others, it is a wasted effort. It then consists merely of the acquisition of detailed knowledge without the ability to transform this into a transforming force to help us realize that we are only in as much as we give ourselves to others. Mother Teresa was not a highly educated individual. I am sure she could not quote Einstein or the classics in the literature. However, what a profound and transcendental impact she had on those around her. She understood the most important equation, truth or intellectual concept. She understood that she was only inasmuch as she served others. This is not to say that we should not pursue intellectual achievements and get a good education for ourselves and family benefit, but we should always keep in mind that this education should also be a vehicle to serve others. May she be our role model.

Another form of intellectual repolarization is found in journalism. Years ago, journalists strived to be objective and impartial. More recently, journalism is being used to bully or bludgeon individuals who hold an opposing opinion. At the beginning, these attempts were subtle in nature and disguised as journalistic opinions. As time passed, however, those engaging in these practices they became blatantly polarized and made no effort to disguise their partiality. This has resulted in the public at large realizing the lack of journalistic integrity, and now sadly it is something that is accepted and even expected, with differing groups reading only the news that agrees with or supports their point of view. The journalists have also fallen prey to their own primal fear of nonexistence, and in order to the defend their own integrative intellectual and social fuels, they resort to attacking different points of view that threaten their own integrative mechanisms. Thus, news, instead of being informative and objective, has become opinionated and supportive of particular perspectives. The fact that the media is able to reach a large segment of the population contributes to social and intellectual repolarization, with the resultant increase in violence among members of opposite-thinking groups. The sad part is that even though journalists contribute to this violence, they refuse to accept their responsibility.

Education can also be used as a mechanism to preserve an ideology by utilizing intellectual polarization. For example, in Cuba, unless people were members of the communist party, they were not able to obtain a higher of education or go into specific careers. By this method, the ruling aristocratic party—in this case, communists—assured themselves that the intellectual class who would wield the power would be made up of individuals who accepted their ideology, and the party relegated those with different ideological points of view to blue-collar jobs that had little or no significant impact on decision making in society. The Communist Youth Party, for example, would go into elementary and middle schools and promote their ideology by promising benefits for those who accepted it.

Another example of intellectual polarization is evident in many universities in the United States. There is an open liberal bias that many people now accept as a reality. If students express conservative views, they may be penalized by their professors and given lower grades. In this way, their opportunities to graduate at a higher level are diminished and their chances of acceptance to higher institutions of learning or obtaining better jobs are decreased. Many students have resorted to keeping their viewpoints under wraps for fear of reprisal. Objective grading is out the window, and ideological grading is the new "in." This is now openly done in many universities without any sense of embarrassment. These professors fall prey to their own fears of nonexistence without clue as to what the driving force is. They have no transcendence, originality, or real depth in their viewpoints, and in essence, they are bound by the same affective fuels as their opponents. Academia, instead of being a bastion for research and new ideas, has become a fortress of ideology. This has led to different universities being labeled as liberal or conservative depending on their slant, with sad consequences to the educational system. The fact that the provosts of these universities have failed to fix this problem only serves to emphasize the moral degradation and perversion of academia.

As in other mechanisms of affective fuels, polarization can take the form of micro- or macropolarization. In the one of the hospitals where I go, a group of doctors were dismissed without due process. The excuse given was that the doctors did not have the necessary training or education to match up to other physicians. Needless to say, this resulted in multiple lawsuits. This education discrimination is an example of micropolarization. Instead of helping these physicians improve their clinical experience, they were segregated. This reflects a profound lack of humanity from individuals who are supposedly educated and should therefore exhibit a high degree of compassion and humanity. On a larger scale, macropolarization takes the form of ideology, which can be then pushed by education and university centers, by journalism, and by movies and other forms of entertainment.

Education as a mechanism of acquisition of other affective fuels plays an important part in society. The more educated individuals are, the higher the incomes they can expect to have. The problem is that their level of education depends, as previously mentioned, not only on the environments in which they are brought up but also on the acquisitive power of the family and whether they are able to pay for a more expensive university for their children. A phenomenon that is taking place now is the advent of robotics, which is displacing a lot of blue-collar workers into the unemployment ranks. Corporations, without regard to the welfare of their employees, are more commonly switching to robotics to perform blue-collar work and manual work. No effort is being made to train employees in the new technology, and this contributes to the segregation of society in terms of intellectual fuel.

The two prior examples of segregation by intellectual fuel in the hospital and the segregation in corporations against blue-collar workers by using robotics points to a worrying trend in society of treating human beings as disposable commodities. Intellectual fuel, instead of humanizing us, is contributing to the dehumanization in our society. Feeding the sense of self and making it feel superior contributes to the segregation in our society.

Education is supposed to give people a higher degree of humanity by making them understand the connection they have not only to other individuals but also to nature. The problem is that education is putting a greater emphasis on technological training and arts training but focusing very little on humanitarian training. The emphasis is on acquiring a technologically advanced education in order to land a good job, without regard to the moral and social responsibilities of one's education. This process contributes to intellectual polarization and, eventually, a schism in society.

The intellectual affective fuel can also lead to polarization by the social affective fuel. As a matter of fact, at times, they are intimately joined. For example, some people suppose that because individuals are African-American or Hispanic, they may have a lower intellectual achievement; this is an example of codependency on social and intellectual fuels. For example, a professor may feel that a student who is Hispanic will submit work that is substandard as compared to that of other students. This leads to a prejudgment that may be reflected in the student's grades. This interdependence stems from the close relationship between social status and intellectual achievement, as explained in a prior paragraph. One thing I learned a long time ago is that there is no monopoly on intelligence. Sometimes, the individual who one expects nothing of is the one who does things that defy imagination. The sooner we realize that we're not special because we have a higher level of education and that the achievement of education has a large component of environmental and circumstantial causes, the sooner we will be able to regard other people with the humanity and compassion that we should have for one another.

Intellectual polarization should not be taken lightly. During the communist revolution of China, education was considered to be a mechanism of polarization or superiority. Many of the working classes sold the intellectuals out as aloof and arrogant, resulting in a purge of educated and intellectual individuals that delayed the recovery of China in scientific and economic ways for decades. The same way that we have physical bullies, we have intellectual bullies.

Another contributing factor to the intellectual polarization has to do with genetics, which affect people's intelligence quotients (IQ). The level of IQ can indicate the degree to which an individual may achieve a higher education in a competitive society and does affect the acquisition of other affective fuels later on in life. A problem that is developing in Europe with the recent influx of immigrants is that, according to some articles, the alleged IQ of the some immigrants is lower than that of the European population. Other articles reflect the fact that a large percentage (82–99%, depending on the source) of this immigrant population still remains unemployed years after immigrating to the country. Putting aside the language and cultural barriers that may affect their ability to find employment; if it is true that they have a lower IQ level, this may hinder their incorporation into a highly technological society. Highly technological societies require a very high degree of education and preparation in order to be incorporated into the work force. Individuals with lower IQ is may find it difficult to compete with native individuals in the country when looking for a job, as the native individual is likely to have a higher level of education and technological training. In the long run, this contributes to polarization by intellectual fuel by limiting this population's ability to obtain high-paying jobs and thus contributing to polarization symptoms in terms of material and social fuels further down the line through the loss of acquisitive power due to the loss of an adequate education.

Questions:

1. What level of education do you have? Does this education make you feel superior or special? Why?
2. How can you use your education to be of service to others?
3. Do you believe that education entitles you to a comfortable life? Once you have achieved material possessions and social status, do you still feel empty inside? Where does this emptiness come from?
4. In your society can you identify intellectual fuels at different levels? Can you see that polarization by intellectual fuels happens in your society? Give examples.

CHAPTER 7

Polarization by Material Fuel

A BUDDHIST STORY tells the tale of a monk who lived very simply in a plain hut and whose only possessions were a mat for sleeping, robes, and a bowl and spoon for his food. Once, a thief came to the hut and stole the bowl. The monk began giving chase. The thief ran across a valley, and the monk ran across the valley; the thief swam across the river, and the monk swam across the river; the thief climbed a mountain, and the monk also climbed the mountain. Finally, the thief was so tired that he turned to the monk and said, "Here's your bowl. Please do not hurt me." The monk looked at the thief perplexed, extended his hand, and said, "I didn't chase you for the bowl. You forgot the spoon."

A similarly themed tale that I heard, recounts a woman who goes to the airport to catch a flight with a container of crackers in her bag. She sits waiting for the flight, and a man sits next to her also with a bag. After a while, she gets hungry, reaches down, and takes a cracker from the bag. A few minutes later, the man sitting next to her reaches down and gets a cracker from the same bag. She notices that and thinks to herself that he is very rude for taking a cracker from her. She reaches down and takes another cracker, and the man after a while does the same. This goes on for some time until only one cracker is left. The man looks down, sees only one cracker left, and does nothing. The woman looks at the cracker, and before he can take it too, she grabs it and eats it. The boarding is called for the flight, and she boards the airplane and sits in her seat. After takeoff, she opens her bag, still upset and expecting to see the empty container of crackers, only to notice that the container is full. She had been eating the man's crackers.

Polarization by material fuel is perhaps the most common form of polarization. Intellectual fuel is described in a prior chapter, and most of the time it leads to polarization by material fuel by affecting the acquisitive power of the individual. This polarization can take place at a micropolarization level or a macropolarization level.

Micropolarization by material fuel occurs within the class system secondary to economic stratification—in this case, rich versus poor. It may be seen beginning in high school, when some students arrive to school in expensive cars, while others have to come by school bus or public transportation. The class system probably begins at this level and becomes more marked as individuals mature. They may feel that they are superior because they have more money than others who have less. The sensation of feeling superior stems from an ego expansion, which makes the self feel more secure against the fear of nonexistence. By comparing themselves to people who have less money, they feel in a way that their existence is assured by this material fuel. It relates all the way back to the fear of nonexistence. At the same time, individuals who are in a lower economic class may start to feel envious (desire of acquisition) of those who they feel have more material fuel, and this may lead to conflict. As these people mature, the class stratification by material fuel becomes more marked. People with more acquisitive power may live in gated communities and enjoy other material benefits, such as cars, houses, social clubs, education, and so on, while those with lower acquisitive power live in more simple houses, have less social entertainment, and have fewer educational chances. Over the course of time, these differences in class lead to a confrontation and the development of different ideological currents.

Thus, we have the development of capitalism and communism. Communism came about as a reaction to what economically disadvantaged people saw as a profound injustice by a richer class. Since, by necessity, the vast majority of individuals have lower acquisitive power than rich people, they grouped together and made a political movement. Based on numbers, this movement eventually overthrew the czarist Russia, and communism began.

Both communism and capitalism essentially suffer from the same malady, which is an attachment to material fuel. Whereas in communism, the desire for acquisition is the driving force, and so strong that it overthrew the rich class, in capitalism the driving forces are twofold: the desire for acquisition as a mechanism of ego integration but also the fear of losing material fuel already acquired. The difference between communism and capitalism is the method in which the material affective fuel of ego integration is acquired. With communism, the government plays a large role in providing the material affective fuel of ego integration. In capitalism, the individuals themselves are the main providers of the affective material fuel.

Both systems suffer from limitations in their approach to obtaining this material fuels. In communism, the government, as mentioned, provides the large majority of material affective fuel by ensuring that no single individual can monopolize these material fuels. The problem with this is that it goes against more than two hundred thousand years of ego evolution. If we understand that the ego is an acquired mechanism of evolution for the species, then the acquisition of material fuel for the sense of self to feel secure goes back more than two hundred thousand years. Communism, by directly providing this material fuel, bypasses the relationship between the self's work and that acquisition. It may also affect people's self-worth since they do not see a direct correlation between their work and the amount of material fuel acquired. The end result is that productivity, which is the result of people's commitment to work to obtain that fuel, is markedly decreased. This decrease in productivity can be seen in all communist countries—for example, Cuba, and more recently, Venezuela, which has gone from a country that produced and exported meat and dairy products to one that now has to import most of its food supply and where hunger is becoming a problem again. By nationalizing private enterprises, the desire for acquisition on which the sense of self bases the productivity was thwarted. People cease to see the correlation between their work and the ability to obtain material fuel, and apathy and lack of productivity ensues. As a result of the loss of material fuel as a mechanism of ego integration, the sense of self will look to a different mechanism of integration and shift the main emphasis of integration from the material fuel to a different fuel, such as social, intellectual, or emotional-sexual fuel. This shift can be seen in Cuba, where, for example, professionals such as female doctors have resorted to prostitution in order to be able to acquire material fuels such as food, clothing, and other benefits. It has also manifested in an increased consumption of alcohol, smoking, partying, social interaction, and promiscuity.

Recently, a world leader form Russia stated that communism is similar to Christianity. This is totally incorrect. While communism is based on the premise that material fuel has to be equally distributed, it does so by imposing or mandating the equalization of that material fuel. In doing so, it is answering to the desire for acquisition on the part of those who lack material fuel. The government is mandating the distribution by a series of laws, and the net effect is an imposition to shape society from the outside in. Christianity, on the other hand, induces the distribution of material fuel by a personal conviction of people who see the union between themselves and the rest of society and are not forced to share what they possess but actually do it motivated by the desire to share. The change comes from the inside out. Under communism, the desire for affective fuels of ego integration is curtailed by an outside force, and this leads to frustration and apathy toward acquisition of affective material fuel, resulting in a stagnant economy. On the other hand, in Christianity, the desire to share does not diminish the desire for affective fuels. As a matter of fact, some people may even feel more motivated to produce in order to be able to share or help more. The net result is that productivity is not impaired. We can surmise, then, that communism is based on the desire for acquisition, whereas Christianity is based on the desire for union.

Pope Francis, during a sermon to mark the Feast of the Epiphany, stated that people "often make do with having health, a little money, and a bit of entertainment," and he urged people to help the poor and the needy communities. He also commented that Christians, "instead of living in coherence with their own Christian faith, followed the principles of the world, which lead to satisfying the inclinations toward arrogance, the thirst for power and for riches." This is commendable, but in order to achieve this ideal, people must be able to understand the mechanism whereby they try to achieve power and material things in the first place. Otherwise, they would continue to be enslaved by these desires that are based on the desire for acquisition from the part of the self to integrate itself against the fear of nonexistence. Only when we understand the mechanism do we have a chance of liberating ourselves from it.

Capitalism is not without its ills, however. The significant divide between the rich and poor classes in capitalist countries generates significant social friction. This is especially true when the rich class utilizes material fuel to put down or humiliate the poor class, leading to more violent conflict and more profound social polarization. If a balance is not found under capitalism so that a strong middle class is developed to serve as a buffer between the rich and poor classes, capitalistic countries tend to eventually drift into communism due to this schism in society. This occurs because the poorer class eventually increases in number to a point where its voting power overwhelms the richer class, which tends to be a minority, and communism is voted in with disastrous consequences for everyone (for example, Venezuela).

A brief example of polarization by material fuels took place recently on British Airways. Passengers are now boarded in order according to the prices of their tickets. These types of micropolarization eventually reach the level of macropolarization as more and more elements of society are segregated according to economic status.

We must understand that in both systems the driving force is a desire for material fuel acquisition to integrate the sense of self against the fear of nonexistence. Socialism seems to be a middle ground between the two. However, it also suffers from the friction noted in capitalism or the apathy found in communism because the pendulum swings from one side to the other. In short, there is no economic or political system within the realm of material fuel that has a significant new way of thinking with regard to material fuel.

Both systems try to maintain their ideological survival by projecting their power into different parts of the world. This desire to maintain their survival is based precisely on the fear of nonexistence by the loss of an ideological and material fuel of ego integration from the individuals who compose the society in which the systems operate. There is no transcendental or profound change or development in the mentality. Both systems are bound by the material fuel of ego integration and have no solutions to this binding. What is needed is a profound realization by which this mechanism operates and a transcendental and fundamental change in the approach to ego integration.

At this point, I think it is worthwhile to analyze the relationships among the different fuels. We have already studied four of them, and we'll need to see the relationships among them. There is an interaction among the social, intellectual, and material fuels. As a matter of fact, all the affective fuels are basically interrelated. They all interplay to support and develop one another. Intellectual fuel is probably the second-most important one behind religious affective fuel. Religious fuel answers directly the fear of nonexistence to the sense of self. Intellectual fuel, however, supports and actually helps to obtain material, social, and emotional-sexual fuel. In a highly technological society like the one in which we live, intellectual fuel serves to obtain economic acquisitive power in order for people to have a house, sustain themselves, have social respect, and eventually marry and have a family. Intellectual fuel, through the development of weapons, also serves to sustain and maintain an ideology. We only need to observe the competition among the world superpowers in terms of projection of military might to understand that intellectual fuel serves to project and diffuse a specific ideology. At the same time, social fuel serves to direct the intellectual fuel in terms of an ideology, and material fuel also directs intellectual fuel in terms of consumerism. In other words, the consumer dictates what innovations and developments intellectual fuel will apply itself to. An example is the mobile phone. Whereas thirty years ago, most phones where attached to a landline, the development of mobile phones increased the available means of communication and sparked a technological revolution. The consumers dictated what applications and what uses the mobile phone eventually came to have. It is easy to see that there is an interplay among all the affective fuels, many of them supporting one another.

In terms of development, the first fuel acquired is the social fuel from the immediate family and friends. The second one acquired is religious fuel, which the family usually teaches to the child. These two fuels serve as the basis of all other fuels that are acquired later. They serve as filters for other fuels that will be processed later. We can think of them as the superego in Freudian terms. The social affective fuel will define what is acceptable or not to people, what is considered to be a sin and what is moral and what is not. In addition, it will serve to establish a sense of priority in terms of what fuels are important to individuals and which are less important. It can be thought of as the base of the other fuels, and it is probably developed in the protoego phase of development. Almost simultaneous with the first two fuels, the intellectual fuel begins to develop. This takes the form of training in kindergarten, elementary school, high school, university, and eventually graduate school. They provide individuals with the acquisitive means to make a living, buy a house, and eventually support a family (material and emotional-sexual fuel acquisition). The priorities to which this intellectual fuel would be applied are guided by the social and religious fuel obtained at an earlier age. So, for example, some individuals might be taught that obtaining material acquisitions (i.e., material fuel) is more important than making a family as a mechanism of integration of the self. These individuals will pursue the acquisition of material fuel at the expense of social and emotional-sexual fuel. An example would be a businessman who sacrifices his personal life in the pursuit of money that he gains. Another individual might be taught that family is the most important factor in his life, so he will pursue making a family over obtaining monetary gains. This religious fuel will dictate the moral parameters within which the intellectual fuel may obtain emotional-sexual and social fuels. The individual may be taught that it is morally right to discriminate against members of a different ethnic or religious denomination and that he may take advantage of them at will, or he may be taught that it is not moral to discriminate or take advantage of anyone. In a very simplistic way of explaining it, this will determine whether the individual steals from other people and becomes a white-collar criminal or if the individual plays fair with other people. In some Middle Eastern countries, it is accepted practice to discriminate against religious minorities, even to persecute them. So as we can see, religious fuel establishes a relativistic moral viewpoint that will be utilized by the intellectual fuel to obtain material, social, and emotional-sexual fuel later in life. Another example would be in cases where the social fuel establishes that homosexuality is prohibited. These individuals would then become less tolerant of individuals who exhibit homosexual behavior. On the other hand, if the social fuel accepts homosexuality, individuals would then be more tolerant of individuals' exhibiting this behavior. One clash going on in Europe right now involves precisely different cultures with different norms of morality regarding the acceptance of homosexuality.

As is evident, intellectual fuel is frequently used for the acquisition of other fuels in most circumstances. In other circumstances, however, intellectual fuel may actually open people's minds and unshackle them from the bonds of the social and religious fuel. If the individuals are courageous enough to challenge the social and religious norms through the application of the intellect, they may then be able to liberate themselves from the values taught to them and explore different venues of affective fuels as a mechanism of integration. It is no surprise, then, that some religious belief systems call it blasphemy or a profound sin to change or question the religious texts. This is a way for the religious establishment to safeguard itself against evolution and to maintain control over the individuals who follow it. It is no surprise, either, that some religious belief systems promise an afterlife full of pleasures (affective fuels for the ego in this reality) to individuals who die defending these religious belief systems. This is a way of manipulating the individuals' fear of nonexistence so that they will die willingly defending the religious belief system. Some religious belief systems even consider the pursuit of higher education to be vanity.

In order for people to liberate themselves from the social and religious fuels, the intellect has to be well grounded, courageous, and open-minded, and people must be willing to face the fear of nonexistence directly, even at the expense of their own selves. Rare is the individual who has this level of courage and is willing to face the primal fear head-on with the realization of his or her own nothingness.

Intellectual fuel appears to have two phases. In one phase is the deductive intellectual fuel that is used for technological training and the sciences and is subject to the acquisition of other fuels. The other phase, which is lesser known, is the inductive or intuitive intellectual fuel that looks into individuals to determine their true nature and liberates them from the mechanisms of affective fuels. Rarer than the individual mentioned above is the society that allows for the development of this openness of thought and is willing to challenge itself in order to evolve socially and religiously.

We can see then that the intellectual fuel is perhaps a two-edged sword—one edge is used to vanquish the so-called enemy and obtain material, social, and emotional-sexual gains, and the other is used to embrace the enemy and dissolve the self. Perhaps one of the biggest breakthroughs in spiritual thinking is the concept of "loving your enemy." This requires an element of humanization that is possible only when we realize our own nothingness not only in ourselves but in others. This concept of loving your enemy has to be understood as a very transcendental one. On the surface, it makes no sense to love someone who is trying to kill you. At a deeper level, we begin to understand that the "enemy" is an individual who has different affective fuels from us and simply wants to protect those fuels. At the same time, the word *loving* relates to the profound realization of our own selves in the other person—in other words, the unity we have with other individual. In this aspect, the enemy is no longer an enemy but another individual with different affective fuel needs who is also governed by the fear of nonexistence and who is trying to integrate his or her own sense of self against that fear by protecting his or her affective fuels by attacking us.

A religious teacher stated that the best cure for depression is to be concerned about other people. There is a profound element of truth in this statement. Let us analyze it carefully. If people have the focus on their own sense of self, then the need for affective fuels and the lack thereof comes to the conscious level. This generates pain and suffering because of the lack of acquisition, the loss of an affective fuel, or the lack of union. The moment that the individuals' focus changes from themselves to other people, the consciousness stops being aware of its own lack of affective fuels and concentrates on helping the other people. In other words, the conscious awareness of their pains disappears. The conscious awareness is focused on other people and on helping them. In observing the pain and suffering of others and trying to help them, individuals many times begin to reflect on their own suffering, realize the unity that they have with the people who are suffering, and begin to transcend their own pain.

Questions:

1. You buy a luxury car. How does this make you feel? What is the mechanism? Is the attention you get from people looking at it sublimated affection? How does this integrate your sense of self?
2. Do you feel superior for having more? Why?
3. Why does ambition never have an end? Does this mechanism apply to other affective fuels? Does promiscuity follow the same mechanism as ambition?
4. After you have obtained material things, you feel empty after a while. When you help others, however, you tend to feel a sense of elation. What mechanism makes you feel like this? How does this relate to a sense of "union"?
5. Materialism is usually attributed to large things. Can materialism also occur on a small scale? Why? What is the mechanism?
6. How does the mechanism of hoarding take place? How does it stabilize the sense of self?

CHAPTER 8

Polarization by Emotional-Sexual Fuel

THE POLARIZATION WE are seeing in society in terms of emotional-sexual fuel can be best appreciated in the conflict between heterosexuals and homosexuals. For starters, let me make a statement: It is totally irrelevant if an individual is homosexual or heterosexual. That is just another mechanism of ego integration. The sense of self will do whatever it takes to integrate itself. In order to understand this polarization, we need to first understand the mechanisms of homosexuality.

In a prior book, *Why Are You? A Sense of Identity*, I explained the mechanisms of homosexuality and also that of fetishes, as well as the relationship between the two. If you feel so inclined to review chapter 9 of that book, you will find a more detailed analysis of this topic. I will try to explain a simplified version of that mechanism in this chapter so that we then can proceed to understand the polarization.

Homosexuality has been assumed to be genetically acquired or environmentally acquired (i.e., nature versus nurture). I ascribe myself more to the environmental pathway as a mechanism of homosexuality. If we assume that it is genetically acquired, then we would have to also explain how people can genetically encode for a fetish, which is explained in the previously mentioned chapter 9 of my earlier book. I will not go into the details of the mechanism of a fetish since it is beyond the scope of this book, but if there is a genetic component, I suspect it is the sensitivity to affection and the need to obtain it were by the sense of self, which will do whatever it takes to obtain that affection.

During the development of the protoego in the child, the child needs the affection of the mother and the father in order to be able to integrate the sense of self. Several stories have come from children who were so deprived of affection in some Russian orphanages that they resorted to a rocking motion and other forms of self-stimulation in order to feel a sense of affection. If children are unable to obtain the affection of the father but perceive that the father loves the mother or that the father is very threatening to them but not the mother, the children will identify themselves with the mother in order to obtain the affection of the father or be less threatening to the dominant figure and ensure their own survival. In the children's minds is the equation, *My father doesn't love me, but my father loves my mother. If I become like my mother, my father will love me.* Alternatively, it may be that the children perceive the dominant figure as a threat and think that, by assuming submissive behavior, they become less of a threat to the dominant figure and ensures their own survival. I have two step nieces, both wonderful girls, who were children to a very dominant father figure. They noticed that their father would pay attention to them whenever they played what are generally classified as boys' sports, such as baseball, volleyball, or soccer. They learned that by exhibiting boy-like behavior, they would garner their father's attention (attention is sublimated affection). Both of them became homosexuals, and they are wonderful human beings.

There might be different mechanisms to homosexuality; the two or three most common ones are the ones described above. The common denominator in all these mechanisms is the self's need for affection, which will adapt its behavior in order to obtain this affection. If the adaptation requires individuals to reject their natural sexuality and opt for an alternative sexuality, individuals will become homosexual. In other words, heterosexuality and homosexuality are essentially behavior mechanisms that integrate the sense of self at a very early age. Since it happens at the level of the protoego, many times, individuals have no control over the behavior since they are trying to integrate their sense of self against the fear of nonexistence. This is why I stated at the beginning that it is irrelevant whether people are heterosexual or homosexual. The mechanism of integration will take place in the most efficient way to integrate the sense of self against the fear of nonexistence and make people feel secure and safe against this fear. Once it is integrated and people learn to obtain affection by this mechanism, it is very difficult to change since that would be tantamount to brainwashing and the basis of the protoego has already been laid down. We can think of this as the base of a building. In order to change the base, you would have to demolish the whole building. The process of conversion therapy is therefore extremely painful because it threatens the sense of self profoundly. This is not to say it cannot be done, but it is painful, costly, and lengthy in its nature.

It appears that the dominant figure in the parental relationship is the one who determines in which direction children will choose to go since that person provides more security to their children. This figure can be either the mother or the father, depending on which one is the dominant figure.

I have a serious concern regarding the "immoral" designation given homosexual behavior by society and religious belief systems. First of all, we must understand that it is an integrative mechanism that depends on the circumstances to which the sense of self is subjected. Any one of us subjected to the same circumstances would wind up the same. If I am able to understand this mechanism and understand that these children have no control over its formation, then how can a deity who supposedly understands everything not understand this mechanism? How can this deity then not love these children as his own? Do you mean to tell me that I understand something that God doesn't understand? Doubtful.

So how does this polarization take place between homosexuality and heterosexuality? The mechanism can be found in the mechanism of prejudice, which was explained in a prior chapter. The sense of self provides for the mechanism of identification, which tends to be subconscious and automatic. If heterosexual individuals are taught that, by identifying themselves with homosexual people, they would become less as determined by the values established by the social and religious fuel, they would actively block and reject homosexual individuals in order to prevent this mechanism of automatic identification from taking place. They would feel that if they identified with homosexual people that they are less—in other words, sustain an ego contraction—and by the same token would feel more threatened by nonexistence. At the same time, homosexual individuals feel rejected in a core mechanism of integration of the self-identity. The reaction would be to lash out and defend that mechanism of integration by reaffirming their sexuality and exhibiting an "in-your-face" attitude and behavior. Both individuals suffer from a fear of ego contraction—one by the fear of identification and one by the fear of rejection of his or her sexual identity core. It must be understood that rejection is the negative of affection and therefore leads to an ego contraction.

The polarization can take place either in a microenvironment—for example, an office or a circle of friends—or in a macroenvironment such as in society, in political groups, and so on.

Promiscuity is an attribute that has been unfairly associated with homosexuality. Promiscuity occur in both heterosexual and homosexual people. The mechanism at its core is essentially that individuals integrate the sense of self and the sexual relationship. After integration takes place, individuals feel comfortable for a while, but afterward the fear of nonexistence reappears, leading them to attempt to stabilize the sense of self with a second relationship. After each relationship, the sense of self is only temporarily stabilized before the fear of nonexistence reappears. This is a repetitive action taken in an attempt to compensate for that fear. Individuals have learned that this compensatory mechanism relieves the fear of nonexistence temporarily, and so it becomes a compulsive behavior. This is the same mechanism as ambition; the only difference is that with ambition, the integration process takes place with material fuel. After each integration with material fuel, the fear of nonexistence reappears and leads to another attempt at integration with more material fuel (cars, houses, money, etc.). Since the fear of nonexistence reappears after each attempt at integration, there is no end to the process; hence the adage that "greed has no limits." So as we can see, promiscuity can occur in both homosexual and heterosexual relationships. An added element in male homosexual behavior may be frustration at being unable to completely assume a feminine role, which would make the desire for compensation with a repeat experience more frequent.

What is needed then is an understanding of the mechanism so that both groups of people—homosexuals and heterosexuals—can understand each other and accept that it is only another integrative mechanism. A compromise between the groups can then probably be achieved in which each group recognizes the other group's fear and necessities and understands that it is our human condition. A very divisive point has been the concept of marriage. Perhaps the various religious belief systems can come up with some sort of definition of a relationship that, although not equal to marriage, may nevertheless recognize the need for union between two partners who truly love each other. And at the same time, the homosexual lobby can seek to understand why heterosexual individuals would feel threatened in their sense of religious integration when they push to legalize religious marriage between them. Compassion and love is needed between both groups and toward each other.

Another mechanism of emotional-sexual polarization is divorce. It would fall under micropolarization because it is usually between two individuals.

What are the causes for a divorce? If we understand a relationship between two human beings in terms of affective fuels, maybe we can clarify why people get divorced. A relationship between two individuals begins with the interchange of affective fuels. Person A may comment on how nice person B looks. Person B may compliment person A or his appearance and his job, and from there, the interchange of affective fuels begins to increase. Both individuals egoes feed off each other at the beginning. This reinforces the sense of self or ego and makes them feel good because they feel safer against the fear of nonexistence. If the relationship stays at this level, it is in danger of eventually falling apart because of the nature of affective fuels. After a while, the mechanism of integration by feeding off the other individual starts becoming ineffectual because, after each integrative process, the fear of nonexistence reappears, leading to another need for reaffirmation of the self from the partner. After a while, the individuals begin to realize that the integrative process has begun to fail, and they seek divorce. On the other hand, if they trascend the affective fuels phase and move into the unity phase, then instead of their focus being on themselves, it will shift to the needs of the other person. At this point true love begins to develop, which is a surrendering of the individual to the other person without regard for his or her own self. Each partner's own self becomes secondary to the needs of the other individual. In this state, they begin to feel less of a need to integrate themselves and more of a desire to help or care for their partners. These relationships tend to last a lifetime.

Some of the ways in which the affective fuels may fail in the affective fuel phase of the relationship are as follows.

- *Failure of social or reinforcement fuel.* One partner may feel that the adulation or compliments he or she is receiving are not integrating him or her or that his or her social life is beginning to be curtailed by this relationship.
- *Failure of economic fuel.* The individuals may run into economic difficulties, and the material integrative mechanism may begin to fail. This leads to aggressivity toward each other, each one blaming the other individually. Eventually, since the mechanism is failing, the couple falls apart.
- *Cheating.* One individual's emotional-sexual fuel may fail to integrate his or her sense of self if he or she becomes bored with the partner. This happens when the emphasis of the sexual relationship is on satisfying or integrating the individual's self and not on surrendering to the other person. Because of the above-explained mechanism of ambition and promiscuity, there is a point where repetitive sexual activities fail to continue to integrate the sense of self. This is when the individual realizes that after each sexual activity, he or she feels as empty as before. The sense or fear of nonexistence reappears after each integration. He or she then tries to obtain a different partner to experience that sense of integration or self-worth. The process repeats itself, and eventually, this could lead to multiple divorces.
- *Intellectual fuel failure.* One partner may feel bored with the other person because their conversation or interaction is not stimulating him or her intellectually. The individual will tend to look for another person who challenges him or her or makes him or her feel that intellectually he or she is achieving something. This again places the emphasis on the sense of self rather than on the other person.
- *Attention on children.* Children may change the dynamics of the relationship, especially when one of the partners takes attention

away from the other partner and gives it to the children. If the individual was feeding his sense of self from the other person, this change in attention (understand, sublimated affection) may lead to an interruption in the affective fuel and may lead the partner to look for a different partner who provides the attention he or she needs. Again, the emphasis is on the sense of self and not on the other person.

- *Religious exclusion.* Religious fuel may also in some cases contribute to divorce. If one of the partners takes refuge in the religious affective fuel to the exclusion of his or her partner, the other partner may feel relegated to second place or ignored, and this may also lead to divorce by the above-mentioned mechanisms. Religion may also sanction abuse, in which case one individual may feel decreased (ego contraction) by this abuse and opt out of the relationship.

As we can see, in human relationships there has to be an evolution from the interaction of affective fuels toward a sense of unity. This only takes place when the two partners realize their own true self in each other and the relationship changes from a psychologically parasitical relationship based on affective fuels to a psychologically giving (selfless) relationship. In other words, they find God in each other in the process of surrendering to each other.

Many people feel a sense of anger after a bitter divorce. To understand the sense of anger, we need to first understand the mechanism of anger. Anger and aggressivity surface when one of three things happens.

- There is some loss or expected loss of an affective fuel of ego integration that—and this is the important part—individuals perceive to be personally directed at them. For example, if a person loses her house to a fire, she may feel depressed but not angry. If, on the other hand, the house is taken away from her to be given to another person, she will experience anger. In the first situation, the fire was accidental and the person, although she experiences a loss of material fuel, will not consider it a direct attack on her sense of integration. On the second occasion, however, the individual perceives the loss of the house as a direct attack on her mechanism of integration. The more acute and more important as a mechanism of integration is the loss of affective fuel, the stronger the reaction will be.

- Lack of acquisition or expected lack of acquisition of an affective fuel with the same characteristics as above
- Breaking down of union

All three mechanisms cause psychological pain as explained in a prior chapter. Several characteristics are common.

- The more acute the loss is, the bigger the reaction will be.
- The more important the affective fuels as a mechanism of integration, the bigger the reaction will be.
- The more the dependence on a particular form of union, whether it be the other individual, the social circle, or the environment, the stronger the reaction will be.

Of course, there is a biological modulating mechanism that inhibits and modulates the anger. And different individuals have different thresholds and modulating biological mechanisms. In general, however, the traditional line between anger and aggressivity is modulated by the above characteristics.

In order to forgive others so that people can continue with their lives, they have to understand the elements of forgiveness as explained in chapter 3. Only when they understand that the other person may have left them due to an inability to integrate themselves with the relationship (ignorance of the process) and relinquish the desire for revenge (desire of acquisition) are they able to move on with their lives. They must understand that the other person may have psychological needs and mechanisms of integration that they may not be able to provide, and that this is not their fault. Since all individuals has their own particular needs of ego integration and these needs change from person to person—and sometimes even change over time—they cannot control the other person's integrative needs and even less their sense of spiritual maturity. As human beings, we are prone to these failings. They must also understand that the divorce itself will cause a loss of affective fuel and an ego contraction. By understanding this mechanism, those affected may be able to forgive the other person and, at the same time, alleviate some of the psychological pain they are experiencing. They are not less because of a personal rejection. The rejection may have nothing to do with the people themselves but with the necessities of integration of the other person. Thus, my advice to individuals going through a divorce is to not take it personally but to understand that, many times, it has to do with the dynamics of the other person independent of their relationship and that they have to be able to forgive in order to move on and rebuild their lives.

Another form of polarization is the phenomenon of "incel," which stands for "involuntarily celibate." The term is used by a group of individuals, usually men, who feel rejected by members of the opposite sex and form a group in which they express their aggression toward women. They use terms like *Stacy* to refer to women who are attractive or desirable and *Chads* to refer to men who are desired by these women, while *Becky* describes an average woman. Their mechanism of ego integration is based upon acceptance by the opposite sex, and when they do not receive this acceptance, they suffer an ego contraction that makes them feel more threatened by nonexistence and become aggressive toward the group that they perceive is rejecting them. A recent massacre in Toronto, Canada, was carried out by an individual who identified himself as an incel. The initial drive is to gain acceptance by the group that they perceive will lead them to an ego expansion, which will make them feel safer against nonexistence. When this does not happen and they feel rejected, they suffer an ego contraction. The ego's mechanism of defense at this point is to reject the entire group, which makes the incels feel "less," induces an ego contraction, and makes them feel more threatened by nonexistence. So they go from a desire to be accepted by a group, aspiring for an ego expansion, to rejection of the group that rejects them, which causes an ego contraction. The sense of self will desire acceptance to induce an ego expansion but will defend itself with rejection when it suffers an ego contraction.

This is a common mechanism of defense of the sense of self. When individuals lack other mechanisms of ego integration and are solely integrated on the affective emotional-sexual fuel, they will respond with aggressivity when they perceive a profound threat to the sense of self by the rejection or lack of acquisition of this fuel.

Several factors modulate this aggressivity.

- lack of other affective fuels of ego integration
- acute loss of emotional affective fuels
- loss of another affective fuel that helped integrate the sense of self
- lack of hope of obtaining an affective fuel
- active rejection by a member of this group with consequent acute ego contraction and an increased feeling of being threatened by nonexistence

When all or some of these factors interact with individuals, they would trigger an aggressive response in order for the sense of self to defend itself from nonexistence. (Convince yourself that nonexistence or nothingness kills.)

Questions:

1. If homosexual behavior is genetic and God created it that way, can he condemn what he created? Would that be fair? Would it be fair to predetermine human beings for condemnation?
2. If homosexual behavior is acquired at the level of the protoego and we understand the mechanism, would God also understand it at a deeper level? Would he have compassion and understanding or not? At the very bottom, what is the motivation of homosexual behavior?
3. You find out your son is homosexual. If you embrace him you have no shadow; if you reject him you have a shadow. Explain.
4. Many religious belief systems espouse the concept of the wife submitting to her husband. This is often misconstrued as the wife being subjected to every whim and wish of the husband.

What is the true meaning of *submission*? Does the husband also have to submit to the wife? Can submission be demeaning or constructive? Explain. When does submission enhance unity? When does submission enhance division?

CHAPTER 9

Anatomy of Tragedies

Juvenile Shootings

RECENTLY IN THE United States, but also in Europe over the last decade, several cases of school shootings by juveniles have occurred. Without going into specific details about the individuals or locations, and without detracting from the personal responsibility and horrendous nature of the crimes, if we examine many of these shootings, we start to see a regular pattern. First, many of the shooters lost parents, either biological or adoptive. This by itself begins to create a problem because individuals are at a very susceptible age when the protoego is being integrated, and if they suffer a profound loss of emotional affective fuel, this causes a shift in the strategy of integration of the protoego to integration into other fuels, such as social, intellectual, religious, or material fuel. Many of these young kids who commit shootings have also encountered rejection in the social fuel. Already burdened with the emotional stress of losing a family member, their behavior is not "normal," according to societal norms. This leads to rejection by their school peers when they're faced with bonding behavior and marks another failure of the integration strategy by the sense of self. This rejection may lead to aggressivity from the individual toward the school, which at that age is the main source of social fuel. To compound the problem even further, many times this rejection by the school "society" also leads to rejection by a girlfriend or female friends. At the adolescent stage, this has a profound effect since it also negates the individual's emotional-sexual fuel. The loss of an emotional affective fuel can be very powerful if an individual who lost his parents is looking for affection from a female friend. Rejection by a girlfriend at a very susceptible pubertal age can trigger a large amount of aggressivity and the desire to lash out at the society that the individual feels is rejecting him and denying him a mechanism of ego integration. Many of these shooters in the past have experienced this rejection at some point or another shortly before the shooting event. With the past failing of the social and emotional-sexual fuels as mechanisms of integration, the young person may be left with no alternative but to try to integrate using a different strategy on the intellectual, material, or religious fuels. Many of these young men also have problems at school due to the emotional trauma that they have experienced and may suffer from a cognitive disability. This further compounds the problem because the individual is not able to feel integrated on the intellectual fuel or to feel a sense of achievement. This leads many times to rejection of the individual by teachers due to behavior problems and further compounds the social affective fuel rejection that he feels. Being young, many of these individuals do not have a complete education as they have not finished college or even high school, and this makes integration to the material fuel difficult. Some of them may have actually lost or were not able to acquire material fuel after the loss of a parent. They may be relegated to work menial jobs that are low-paying, and they may even be abused by their cohorts. Many of these young people do not have a religious fuel that could serve as a barrier to violence. This throws the door to violence wide open when the individual feels that his integrative mechanisms are failing or are being taken from him against his will. The social rejection may also push them into looking for extreme ideologies like, for example, Nazi or other radical groups that may advocate violence. The ideology itself may not be the drawing factor, but the sense of acceptance (social fuel) and affection that they derive from being accepted into the group will be. The group itself may comprise other individuals with similar problems who have experienced similar rejections, and the aggressivity that they express is then transmitted to the young person. This sets the stage for violence since it is the only mechanism the individual has learned to protect himself from the lack of integration to the absence of affective fuels, which he feels have been taken from him. In essence, the individual is now a time bomb. It only takes a small trigger—for example, the rejection of a girlfriend or another public rejection—to make him cross the threshold into active violence and a massacre. If we look at many of the school shootings, some of the many common denominators are the lack of affective fuels, the loss of affective fuels, and social rejection not only by their peers but also by the school system, and especially by their girlfriends as triggering factors. Understanding that victims are not to blame, and without detracting from the horrendous nature of the crime or the personal responsibility of the perpetrator, possible solutions to this problem is to actively identify these young people and educate the school's staff and the student body about the need to be compassionate and tolerant. People do not develop aggressivity toward others who help and accept them. In other words, animals do not bite the hand that feeds them.

Social Shootings

Social media has also been the cause or the triggering factor for some shootings. One only needs to look into the news to find examples of this. Social media is predominantly social affective fuel. Whereas before it existed, people would have a small circle of friends and the rejection by the group was limited, with social media, people may have thousands of followers and the rejection is thus magnified. Social media can also be used to obtain material fuel. Many times, individuals will integrate themselves solely on social media and the material fuel that they obtains from it to the exclusion of other fuels. Recently on April 2018, a video streaming company in the United States was the site of such violence. If individuals are mostly integrated on the social affective fuel as a mechanism of obtaining identity and at the same time derive material fuel in the form of revenues from that integration through the media, interruption of this social fuel may lead to a profound ego contraction and threaten the individuals' sense of identity or self, to which they will react with aggressivity. If individuals have no religious, emotional-sexual, or intellectual fuels as mechanisms of integration, failure of the social and material fuels may lead to violence. Analysis of violence perpetrated in response to social media can be seen from this perspective. The social affective fuel will substitute the emotional-sexual fuel in the sense that it is a form of sublimated affection. The material fuel provides for sustenance and economic maintenance. Again, if no religious fuel is present to provide a barrier against violence, if the individuals have no partners or significant others to provide them with emotional-sexual fuel, and they're not integrated in their achievements, then limiting the social fuel may lead to a profound ego contraction since it has become the main mechanism of integration. Many of the acts of violence related to social media can be traced to this combination of factors and the fact that the main integrative mechanism of the sense of self becomes social media to the exclusion of others.

Suicide over Bureaucracy

Recently, there was a case report by of a young man in the UK who committed suicide because of an unpaid traffic ticket that led to the loss of his motorcycle, his mode of transportation. Again, we can see how integration into a sole affective fuel can lead to depression and an act of violence. If individuals are integrated mainly on a material fuel subset—in this case, transportation—and lack all other integrative fuels, the loss of this material fuel will lead to a profound ego contraction. For example, if an immigrant has a lemonade stand as a means of obtaining economic fuel to maintain his family and also develop a sense of self-achievement, the closure of the lemonade stand may lead to the loss of not only the material fuel he needs for sustenance but also his status (social fuel) and affection and self-esteem (emotional-sexual fuel). Again, if no religious fuel is present as a barrier to suicide or violence, then the individual may be willing to commit an act of violence or suicide in retaliation for what he perceives is the taking away of an affective fuel of ego integration. If the individual perceives that what he was doing was against the law but nevertheless loses the affective fuel, he may not develop aggressivity but go into a depression because he does not perceive the loss of affective fuel to be directed at him personally. In other words, he doesn't feel it is a direct attack. On the other hand, if the loss of affective fuel is felt to be an unfair and direct attack against him, then outward aggressivity will develop. I have spoken on some of the above examples regarding the presence of religious fuel as a barrier to violence. We need to understand that if religious fuel prohibits violence, then it can also act as a strong barrier against it. This is so because the religious fuel, as mentioned in prior chapters, is the most powerful fuel because it directly answers the fear of nonexistence. If, on the other hand, the religious belief system condones violence as a mechanism of conflict resolution, then there would be a propensity for violence. By condoning violence, the religious belief system essentially conveys to the individual that violence will not impair his acceptance into the afterlife, or whatever his belief of existence after death may be. This would make the individual more prone to use it. An example of how this can happen can be found in many areas of the Middle East, which has been plagued by violence for the more than 1000 years. In the example that we are discussing of the young man who committed suicide, the lack of a religious belief system may have opened the door to that act.

By committing suicide, the individual essentially turns off the ego, which is the source of pain and the reason he feels threatened by nonexistence. This is the source of suicidal thoughts, a desire to turn off the ego so that there is no more ego contraction or fear of nonexistence. Again, the paradox is that the individual prefers to embrace nonexistence rather than to live with the fear of it.

We have to understand that the fear of nonexistence is real. It is difficult to see, but if people follow their fears and insecurities backward and continue to ask why every single time they realize them, they will eventually reach a point where there is no answer. At this point, if they continue to push, they will eventually see the fear that underlies the mechanism.

Observe that in both cases described above, attention is sublimated affection. Attention, whether negative or positive, is still a form of affection. That's why the concept of "affective" fuels of ego integration makes sense. The loss of generalized attention such as the kind that is acquired from social media, where thousands of people give likes, has a big impact on the sense of self and integration of the sense of self on social media. Whereas before, individuals may have been liked or disliked by a small group of people, with social media, thousands of people may like or dislike them, and the impact is much stronger. This is why social media is so addictive: it works like drugs and alcohol as a mechanism of integration based on social affection. If individuals push this concept of integration based on affection to an extreme from an evolutionary point of view, we could even theorize that, as a mechanism of evolution, individuals who are given affection by their parents have a better mechanism of integration than those who are abandoned or rejected by their parents. Individuals who received affection would be better equipped to survive in and adapt to the environment than those who lacked affection. One can even theorize that this may be a mechanism whereby parents who were not very caring or loving with their offspring are prevented from further reproducing since the offspring may not be as adaptable to the environment and have lower chances of survival. This may be a way of preselecting parental behavior that is loving and caring over parental behavior that is not.

Shooting Induced by Emotional Rejection

Another tragedy that befell the United States was a shooting in Texas in which people were killed by a high school student. There are many examples of this. Again, we saw the same common denominators. As was reported on the news media, Nazi propaganda and gun propaganda were found that glorified the use of violence and a feeling of superiority in those holding these beliefs. Apparently, in school, the shooter experienced rejection by the other students and some of the sports coaches—the same pattern of social rejection and of the individual's turning to a culture that makes him feel superior and promotes violence as a mechanism of feeling superior. The emphasis on guns is a mechanism whereby the individual felt protected from the fear of nonexistence that was caused by the rejection of the students around him (lack of social fuel). In addition, intellectual achievements are not a mechanism of integration. With no religious fuel, there is no barrier to violence, and there was no well-paying job or mechanism of material fuel integration. And finally, the shooter faced rejection from a girl in public, which constitutes social rejection as well as emotional-sexual rejection. Again, we see the lack of integrative mechanisms to protect the sense of self from nonexistence; the reliance on an alternative social fuel, such as Nazism, to make the shooter feel superior to the other students; and the tilt toward guns and violence as a mechanism of feeling protected from the threat to the lack of affective fuels that the individual experiences. The triggering factor appears to be the rejection from the girl and then the acting up on the belief system that made the individual feel superior as a way of reinforcing his sense of self.

In all these tragedies, the media inadvertently plays a part, contributing indirectly by providing media coverage and publicity. This constitutes attention (albeit negative attention, which is sublimated affection) and gives the individual the affective fuel that he craves in the form of social fuel to stabilize the sense of self. The individual is hungry for an affective fuel of ego integration and obtains it indirectly from the media.

The Case of the Woman behind the Sheets

The following case is not a tragedy, but it is a very interesting case that I came across and that also serves to explain the mechanisms of affective fuels as they interact with our behavior. The case was presented to me by a nurse in one of the hospitals where I work because she was curious about why the individual did what he did. She explained to me that her father-in-law was a very flirty person, especially with her. He would make sexually oriented comments to her, and sometimes she would also flirt with him and make comments back to him. She was very attentive and kind with him. One day he confided in her that the thing that excited him most when he was in a relationship with a woman was when the woman would hide behind a sheet with a small hole in it and peek at him through the hole. Neither he nor she could understand why this would excite him. As part of the background, she explained to me that her father-in-law's father was a very violent and aggressive individual. He used to beat him and his mother. He also confided in her that at one point he had had sexual relations with another man but that he would always give the sex; he never received it. He was also very insistent on her changing her maiden name to his family name. She could not understand this behavior. If you are a psychiatrist or psychologist, I suggest that you stop reading here for a few minutes and try to figure out the mechanism for this behavior before you continue reading.

Ready? To understand this behavior, we must first understand that several clues are given about the affective needs of this individual. First, the fact that he had an aggressive father probably meant that he felt threatened by him and used the mechanism of identification to try to obtain attention or affection from him. Second, the fact that he had engaged in sexual relations with men also points to the mechanism of identification. When he was having this relationship with a man, he was identifying himself with a man receiving the sex. In other words, he was reacting with another man through the process of identification with the man receiving the sex. This is probably because, in his upbringing, he had social and religious fuels that block the overt manifestation of homosexuality. But why the excitement with the woman behind the sheet? To understand this, we have to realize that the sheet essentially serves to hide the identity of the person on the other side. Holding the sheet between them allows for the individual or the other person to look at him and express an interest in him. What gets him excited is the attention or interest that he perceives the other person has in him. This represents the need for affection and interest from his father that he did not have when he was a child. The sheet covers the identity of the woman, which makes it easier for him to perceive her as a male rather than a woman. Doing so makes the fantasy of the father paying attention to him more real. In essence, he is looking for the attention and affection of his father that he did not receive when he was a child in order to integrate his sense of self. The figure behind the sheet is not a woman, then, but an undefined figure who pays attention to him. That could easily be transposed onto his father. The excitement comes from receiving attention. The fact that he wants his daughter-in-law to change her name to his family name also points to a desire to make her part of his family because, that way, the mechanism of identification with her also becomes easier. The fact that she was flirting with him reveals that she was giving him attention and affection. Having her maiden name changed to his family name makes it easier for him to identify with her since his family name is obtained from his father and thus facilitates the mechanism of identification with her also.

Jonestown Massacre: Cult Psychology

Examining the Jonestown massacre also gives us insight into the affective fuel mechanisms and how they can serve to explain that horrible tragedy. First, let's consider some background (obtained from Wikipedia, other Internet sources, and media reports from that time). The leader of the cult, Jim Jones, was a white minister who preached unconventional socialist and progressive ideas to a mixed white and African-American congregation. It was reported at the time that his father was an alcoholic, which leads us to suspect that Jones's father probably wasn't very caring toward him and may have even been aggressive toward him. This may have triggered a need for acceptance or reaffirmation of the sense of self (emotional-sexual fuel). He went through a financial crisis that forced the family to move, and this probably triggered his interest in communism and Marxism as a way to deal with the fears of financial instability (material fuel). He was drawn to Pentecostal churches, where he desired acceptance (religious fuel) and was further rejected by his father when he brought an African-American friend to his house once (social fuel). The friendship he had with this friend provided him with the acceptance and affection that he lacked from his father. Many Pentecostal churches also have mixed white and African-American membership, which also provided him with the acceptance and affection he needed (social fuel). He had an interest in death, having apparently once stabbed an animal to death, and performed funerals for animals. This is a little bit harder to understand. We may surmise or speculate that the fascination with death may have resulted either from a desire to escape his painful reality by identifying himself with the animal being killed or dying (the pain stops when the sense of self is killed) or from a desire for union through death. This last concept of union through death is more difficult to grasp. Some religious belief systems profess that, in death, believers find total union with the absolute and feel complete again. Intuitively, or subconsciously, many people are able to grasp this concept. Through his participation in Pentecostal religions, Jones may have discovered the ability to manipulate people since religion is the most powerful affective fuel because it directly answers the fear of nonexistence by guaranteeing existence after death. In addition, by manipulating this fuel, he was able to obtain people's attention and feel accepted, which is what he craved. Attention is sublimated affection, as I have explained before. This led him to establish a church where he preached Marxism and racial equality and demanded absolute loyalty from his followers. The fact that he craved acceptance and attention so much is the reason a betrayal would be so painful to him (social fuel). As the group grew, there was the process of affective fuel quantification, in which he reasoned that if one person admired him and paid him attention (sublimated affection), then eight hundred people would pay him eight hundred times more attention and affection. On the other side of the equation is the group of individuals that followed him. At a time when prejudice and racism were prominent, an individual preaching racial equality would appeal to many people suffering from these indignities. Likewise, in difficult economic times, his emphasis on Marxism and communism would also appeal to many people suffering from economic hardship. Religion allowed him to manipulate these people's fears by promising them equality and compensation with treasures or the end of hardships in the afterlife. The cult began to become family to many people. It provided interaction and acceptance (social fuel), sustenance and shelter (material fuel), a religious belief system (religious fuel), an education and an ideology (intellectual fuel), and finally access to members of the opposite sex within the group who can intermarry (emotional-sexual fuel). By providing all these fuels, the cult was essentially feeding the affective fuels of ego integration that the followers needed in totality. And Jones didn't have to go out and look for these affective fuels himself because the cult was already providing them. This is why he had such a great dependency on the members of the cult, especially if they had difficulty obtaining these affective fuels outside. The need for acceptance and loyalty is a big factor to the leader of a cult. Once the individual tastes the social affective fuel and emotional-sexual fuel in large quantities, the sense of self becomes integrated on them, making it very difficult to wean the self from them. The self would react aggressively to any perceived betrayal since that would be interpreted as a threat to the social and emotional-sexual fuel on which it is integrating itself. This is why Jones reacted somewhat aggressively when people would betray him or questioned his church. Faced with the prospect of a congressional investigation, of the dissolution of his church, and losing face in front of his people (loss of affective social fuel), he elected to order their mass suicide instead—probably in his mind maintaining the sense of union in the afterlife. Remember that fragmentation of union is one of the sources of psychological pain. The members of the cult who followed his orders did so out of fear of losing the social fuel, the acceptance, and all the other fuels that the cult had provided them. Rather than be faced with the prospect of having to look for these affective fuels themselves, they opted to drink the poison in the belief that they would continue to receive them and be together with other members of the cult in the afterlife. This explains their blind loyalty and adherence to the cult.

Heaven's Gate Cult

The same analysis can be made about Marshall Applewhite, the head of a group called Heaven's Gate that committed mass suicide in California. Based on information obtained from Wikipedia, other Internet sources, and news media reports at the time, the underlying mechanisms of the cult reveal the same pattern. First, there is the social affective fuel in the sense that people have a community that accepts them. The leader of the group becomes a parental figure and is endowed with authority through the acceptance of the group. In turn, the members desire his acceptance as a mechanism of parental affection. Thus, it becomes very easy for him to control the rest of the group. Second, there is an element of religious belief—in this case, the belief that an extraterrestrial UFO would come, rescue the people from their present lives, and usher them into new bodies. This is the religious belief system that directly answers the fear of nonexistence. Third, the community provides an intellectual ideology based on their beliefs. Fourth, they provide the members with housing and food, and fifth, they also provide emotional-sexual fuel in the form of companionship between males and females with the same belief system.

If you have any doubts that this cult's manipulation of people has to do with the fear of nonexistence, you only have to look at the belief system in detail to observe that it directly gives an answer to that fear. The cult members believed that the earth was about to be recycled and that their human bodies were only receptacles. They believed that, in order "to be eligible for membership in the Next Level, humans would have to shed every attachment to the planet." This meant that all members had to give up all human-like characteristics, such as their families, friends, sexuality, individuality, jobs, money, and possessions. Observe at this point that the members were giving up all the affective fuels of ego integration. They also believed that there was an evolutionary level above human (TELAH) in which humans would derive energy from the sunlight and live in eternal bliss (the concept of bliss is conveniently not defined). They also believed in beings called Luciferians that prevented humans from evolving and that they themselves were beings with carnal bodies that had stopped trying to progress.

According to the Heaven's Gate cult, there were several processes whereby a human could graduate to the next level. As can be surmised from different sources it appears that the ability to graduate to a different level depended of several factors (this may or not be fully accurate)

1. Abduction by a UFO. The individual would then be transformed or changed
2. Natural death or death by violence, whereby the individual would ascend to the next level.
3. Persecution that leads to death. (This is probably in reference to the Waco tragedy in Texas). This would be another form of the soul, graduating to the next level.
4. Suicide

On March 22 and 23, 1997, thirty-nine members committed suicide.

Observe the importance of an afterlife for this particular cult. This attachment to an afterlife is a direct response to the fear of nonexistence that I have been referring to all throughout the book. It is also present in other religions, with the difference that in some religious belief systems, it not actively sought, while in others the precondition of an act of violence is necessary to enter the afterlife in an agreeable way. If fear of nonexistence were not present, there would be no reason for this cult to dwell so heavily on this concept.

The same analysis can be made with regard to the 1993 tragedy in Waco, Texas. It appears that emphasis on a religious belief system and an afterlife was predominant in that cult. In addition, the pursuit of emotional-sexual fuel in the form of intercourse with several people and the leader, David Koresh, was reported in the media. The desire for power (social fuel) and respect appeared to influence the leader heavily. Again, we see the necessity for social and emotional-sexual fuels as an integrative mechanism. During his childhood, according to Wikipedia, Koresh was abandoned by his father, who ran away with a teenager, and his mother eventually married a violent alcoholic. At this point, the necessity for social acceptance and, at the same time, emotional-sexual fuel as a mechanism of ego integration may have begun developing. Religion became a mechanism whereby he could manipulate others and obtain the necessary integrative fuels that he craved due to the lack of them during his childhood.

All throughout history, religion, in one form or another has been used to manipulate individuals, and the power that it exerts, as mentioned before, is primarily due to the fear of nonexistence that we all have as a price to pay for existing. By manipulating the concept of an afterlife, individuals can be persuaded to die for their religious belief system and even kill for it in order to achieve what they consider to be an afterlife. Needless to say, if we objectively analyze this behavior, we realize that as long as individuals are concerned with their own salvation, there is in essence a selfish desire. The question I pose to the reader is this: Let us suppose that your child is going to be condemned by God, and you have the chance to face eternal damnation in his or her place so that your child could be saved. Would you, out of love, accept eternal damnation for your soul so that you could save your child? Interestingly, only one figure has done this according to religious texts among the many religious belief systems, and he did it for all of us.

Shooting Induced by the Media

Another situation that merits discussion is shootings that are induced by media publications. This happened in France, where the staff of a satirical magazine was attacked, as well as in the United States at a more individual level more recently. For example, if an individual is categorized by the media as a stalker or a pervert and judicial proceedings are published that show his guilt, the individual may be curtailed from obtaining all the affective fuels due to this publicity. He may find it hard to obtain emotional-sexual fuel because members of the opposite sex will now be afraid of him. If the individual has an affective dependency or need for this affection due to the lack of it during his childhood, this may affect him profoundly. In addition, the publicity adversely affects his chances of obtaining material fuel since employers will be less inclined to give him a job. Intellectual fuel may also suffer since universities will think twice about admitting him to pursue a degree because of their liability to other students. And social fuel will also suffer because he may be ostracized or rejected by others. The individual may try to retaliate legally against the media, but if this fails, he may feel that the only recourse he has is violence. Again, the lack of religious fuel, acting as a barrier against violence, may be a contributing factor. In short, we can see how adverse publicity against an individual, even if it is correct, may impact this individual's mechanism of integration so severely that he may feel extremely threatened and react with violence.

Social Media Suicide

One needs only to look at the news on the Internet to find multiple examples of suicide induced by social media. (Different from media publications) Cases have been reported involving young people who have shared a private matter with friends only to have it publicized widely on social media and the Internet. On several occasions, these young people have found themselves in trouble with the law or the universities they were attending when their private matters were shared publicly. If young people, for example, engage in a sexual indiscretion with another friend and this is shared publicly on social media, it may lead to their being ostracized and even expelled from a university. If the individuals are integrated mostly on the intellectual fuel as a mechanism of obtaining other fuels in the future (for example, a career or job and eventually a home, spouse, and family), they may suffer a profound ego contraction when this occurs, which may lead to a loss of hope in the future or in their aspirations, and this may lead to suicide. Educational institutions have to be aware of the profound impact that expelling students from the university or educational center carries. In a society where intellectual achievement (intellectual fuel) is the main mechanism of ego integration, it can lead to devastating consequences. Highly technological societies depend on integration on the intellectual fuel as a mechanism of obtaining other fuels. This is not the case with more primitive societies, where subsistence farming, agriculture, or artisanship is the main mechanism of obtaining other fuels. If individuals have been educated since childhood to think that intellectual achievements by the mechanism of integration by the social filter (social fuel) are critical, then failure to earn a degree (lack of acquisition as described in a prior chapter) may have profound adverse consequences on the mechanism of ego integration and lead the individual into profound ego contraction and suicide.

In chapter 2, I explained that an ego contraction can take place due to the loss or expected loss of an affective fuel. This is an example of an expected loss causing an ego contraction and the subsequent psychological pain. We could argue that the ignorance of these mechanisms by the law and educational institutions and its effects on people can lead to this tragic end and that the matters can be handled in a different way, perhaps by counseling and private meetings between the affected parties, to lead to a different outcome. We sometimes do not realize that we are dealing with human beings and that our actions have a profound impact on the psychology and behavior of people. At some point, the element of forgiveness has to start playing a role in all these interactions.

In view of these common denominators, it makes sense to try to devise a table to gauge the amount of polarization or radicalization that an individual may be prone to. We can do this in terms of affective fuels. Researchers and law enforcement personnel are welcome to do research on this table, modify it, and adjust it as needed and then see if it helps to prevent polarization and radicalization and perhaps acts of violence in the future.

TABLE 2. Polarization/radicalization index in terms of affective fuels

Social Fuel		
1. Exposure to a social fuel that is permissive of violence or advocates violence as a mechanism of conflict resolution	Protoego stage (3–5yrs) ---- Adult stage ---------	2 points 1 point
2. Exposure to a culture of superiority or that discriminates against others	Protoego stage (3–5yrs) ---- Adult stage --------------	2 points 1 point
3. Rejection by society or a group of individuals that people consider to be their society (e.g., students, host culture in the case of immigrants)	Protoego stage (3–5yrs) --- Adult stage --------------	2 points 1 point
4. Social belief system that blocks integration into a native or host culture adult stage	Protoego stage (3–5yrs) ---- Adult stage --------------	2 points 1 point
5. Social isolation into a cultural ghetto as a mechanism to avoid integration into a host culture	Protoego stage (3–5yrs) --- Adult stage --------------	2 points 1 point
6. Gang participation to obtain "respect"	Protoego stage (3–5yrs) ----- Adult stage --------------	2 points 1 point

Religious Fuel

1. Exposure to a religious belief system that promotes violence against individuals who do not believe the same	Protoego stage (3–5yrs) --- Adult stage ------------	2 points 1 point
2. Exposure to a religious belief system that discriminates against individuals who do not hold the same belief system or makes people feel superior for their belief systems	Protoego stage (3–5yrs) ---- Adult stage -------------	2 points 1 point
3. Exposure to a religious belief system that blocks integration into a native or host culture due to a fear of condemnation (understand fear of nonexistence)	Protoego stage (3–5yrs) ---- Adult stage ---------------	2 points 1 point
4. Belonging to a religious group or gang to maintain a sense of identity in a foreign culture	Protoego stage (3–5yrs) ----- Adult stage ---------------	2 points 1 point

Intellectual Fuel

1. Exposure to intellectual fuel makes people feel superior or discriminate against those who are less educated	Protoego stage (3–5yrs) ---- Adult stage -------------	2 points 1 point
2. Lack of integration in an intellectual fuel that provides for means of obtaining other fuels	Adult stage -----------	1 point

Material Fuel

1. Integration in a belief that material fuels make people superior to others	Protoego stage (3–5yrs) ---	2 points
	Adult stage -------------	1 point
2. Lack of integration or lack of availability of material fuel for integration	Extreme poverty --------	2 points
	Poverty ---------------	1 point

Emotional-Sexual Fuel

1. Participation in an illicit gang or group of individuals that promotes acceptance, friendship, respect, and facilitation of sexual favors		2 points
2. Recent loss of a significant other, rejection by a girl or boy, or feeling ostracized by a member of the opposite sex		2 points
3. Recent loss of immediate family, such as a father, mother, brother, or sister		2 points

Aggravating Factors

| 1. Lack of multiplicity of affective fuels of ego integration with integration exclusively on one affective fuel that is lost | | 2 points |
| 2. Prior use of violence as a mechanism to obtain affective fuels | | 2 points |

3. Passivity of host culture toward violence against its laws and established social principles; lack of protection of host population by the government		1 point
4. Inability of a host government to provide a mechanism of integration for nonnatives of the host culture		1 point
5. Lack of enforcement of integration into the culture, even to the point of accepting behavior contrary to the laws of the country (for example, discrimination against gays and women)		1 point
6. Identification with a religious or social group that is perceived to be under attack when the main mechanism of integration of the individual is precisely its identification with that group		2 points
7. Acute loss of the main integrative fuel of ego integration (whichever it may be)		2 points

The higher that people score on these tables, the higher the probability that they will become radicalized or polarized in society. I have given more weight to characteristics obtained at the protoego level (between three to five years) because that time is when a sense of self is beginning to form and the social and religious filters are incorporated into the sense of self. Once people have been formed on the social or religious belief systems, changing them becomes very difficult. They would experience a profound crisis of identity that would be psychologically painful since they would feel they were becoming less in the process of losing those social or religious belief systems. Our natural tendency is to attach ourselves to them and defend them against perceived attacks. That is why theocratic and political regimes put so much weight on indoctrinating individuals at a very young age, and it's why it is so important to raise young people on social and religious belief systems that are based on tolerance, compassion, and unity rather than on discrimination and segregation. Recently, an article discussed a terrorist group (ISIS) in the Middle East that committed multiple atrocities and that has been almost completely defeated. In the article, the author explained how the terrorist group had shifted its strategy from obtaining land and controlling territory (material fuel) to indoctrinating younger people to ensure their ideological existence after their defeat.

One must understand that these mechanisms are all attempts of the self to maintain its integrity and defend itself against the fear of nonexistence. They all go against a sense of universal union since, in that universal union, the sense of self is somewhat lost. They may, however, accept selective union provided that that union protects their respective affective fuels of ego integration.

CHAPTER 10

Where Do We Go from Here?

> Watch your thoughts, for they become words. Watch your words, for they become deeds. Watch your deeds, for they become habits. Watch your habits as they become character. Character is everything.
>
> —Chinese proverb

WE ARE OUT of time, and the situation is dire. We are headed toward a major war due to the polarization mechanisms that I have described. The Buddhists have a saying: "Emptiness is form, and form is emptiness." This saying is true and can be understood by looking at it closely and experiencing it. There is another side to it, though. Emptiness or nonexistence is simultaneously the most constructive and destructive force in the universe. As we can see from the prior chapters, fear of nothingness, or emptiness, is the driving force behind the sense of self. It is the price we pay for what we achieve (self-consciousness). If we exist, we can stop existing. The sense of self strives to reaffirm its existence by the five main affective fuels and their subsets. When the desire to reaffirm existence is done in a constructive way, such as by realizing ourselves socially, intellectually, materially, religiously, and emotionally, the result is a constructive process in which society as we know it advances forward. As individuals, we tend to reaffirm our existence by the affective fuels, and this results in intellectual, material, and social achievements. I am sitting here now in a hotel room in Orlando looking at massive hotel that is the result of the interdependence of many individuals—financiers, architects, engineers, technicians, laborers, designers, chemical and metallurgy industry workers, so on and so on. Each of these individuals tries to answer that fear of nonexistence by the realization of him- or herself as a professional as well as a family member and a member of society. The outcome is a community effort that results in the development of such beautiful buildings. The same holds true for other facets of our society. The interdependence that we have is our biggest asset, and within that interdependence, we function as individual units striving to realize ourselves and reaffirm our existence by contributing to that unitary effort. The fear of nonexistence drives us to try to realize ourselves and reaffirm our existence by the different intellectual, material, and other achievements, all of them based on the affective fuels of ego integration.

The opposite is also true: nonexistence can also be a destructive force. Several mechanisms may lead to this.

- Individuals may lack the mechanisms to integrate themselves against this fear, which may lead to psychological aggressiveness since they may feel the threat of nonexistence. They may feel like a corralled animal and respond aggressively toward the society around them, which they feel may have been the cause of their angst. An example can be seen in the mass shooting in Parkland, Florida.

- If individuals have affective fuels that come into conflict with affective fuels from a different group of individuals, they may feel threatened and react with aggressive, destructive tendencies in order to protect themselves. For example, some religious belief systems profess that people who do not believe like they do have to be killed or destroyed. By not following this command, they may believe that they will be condemned to eternal hellfire and, out of a fear of nonexistence, they act on this belief system by committing genocide and acts of terrorism.

- Through the process of identification, individuals may identify with a particular social or religious group and reinforce their sense of identity based on this identification. If they perceive that that particular social or religious group is under attack, they may react aggressively against what they perceive to be an aggressor even though the attack is not directed toward them specifically. Theocracies in the Middle East suffer from this problem because, many times, they block the acquisition of affective fuels. By blocking, for example, mechanisms of joy like parties and social gatherings, emotional manifestations like holding hands and hugs, social interactions between males and females, and liberal thinking in intellectual achievements unless it concurs with the line of thought of the theocracy, they essentially block the ability of the sense of self to integrate itself on anything other than a religious belief system. To further complicate the issue, this religious belief system promises the sense of self—precisely what they block in reality—in the afterlife. This leads to people becoming obsessed with obtaining them in the afterlife with the precondition of committing an act of violence. This leads to massacres and intolerance. To say that many of these so-called religious teachers lack a profound understanding of human nature is an understatement. They pretend to teach others about God, but they cannot even see the hand of God in themselves.

• Ideologies, many times inflexible in their application, may try to promote themselves as superior precisely to fight against the fear of nonexistence. This may lead to the elimination of those who they consider to be inferior so as to prevent the mechanism of identification. For example, look at Nazi Germany and the Holocaust they perpetrated, which was one of the greatest tragedies of all times. This was done because they believed in a superior race, and they thought that by eliminating those who they considered to be inferior, they would be able to achieve it. The driving force behind them was a profound fear of nonexistence, which they thought to counter by feeling superior to others and in doing so reaffirming their existence. If one associates being inferior or smaller to an ego contraction, which gets you closer to nonexistence, then the opposite, feeling superior, corresponds to an ego expansion, which protects you from nonexistence.

Hence we can see that nothingness is simultaneously constructive and destructive depending on how individuals try to compensate for this fear of nonexistence or what their mechanism of ego integration is against this fear.

The problem that we have is that as, population density increases, there is a convergence of communities with different affective fuels of ego integration. Instead of realizing that the sense of self is a learned evolutionary process that is flexible and not fixed, we tend to take the sense of self as something solid and feel threatened when we are exposed to individuals with different affective fuels. This convergence in society is increasing the number of conflicts by bringing people with different affective fuels into contact. That makes us feel threatened by one another as we question whether the affective fuels that we have for integration are the correct ones or not. We tend to defend those we have since we fear that if we lose them, we will become less and feel more threatened by nonexistence. This conflict will continue to increase and eventually lead to an all-out war unless we begin to understand the mechanisms of ego integration and become able to transcend these mechanisms. I'm afraid that it is already too late to be able to revert this process. Unfortunately, we may have to endure a war in which billions will die in order to realize that we need to change. The change cannot be brought about by exterior forces, like many leaders have suggested. It has to come from a sincere and genuine desire to change from within. The change has to come from the inside out, not from the outside in. The change can only take place if we understand the need for affective fuels and take steps to liberate ourselves from them and to control them. Governments cannot impose affective fuels because all they do is regulate their acquisition, not the necessity that we have for them. The necessity we have for them can be changed only from the inside with a profound understanding of these mechanisms. As a very famous physicist, Dr. Hawkins, who led an exemplary life against tremendous adversity and who should be our role model, once said that we need to reach the stars if we are to survive as a species. As much as I admire him, I have to disagree with him. Unless we profoundly change the way we understand ourselves, all we would do if we reach the stars is bring with us the same problems, the same conflicts, and the same wars, and the process would start all over again on a different planet. We need to profoundly change our conception of the self and accept with humility that we are not all that we think we are and then some. When we start understanding that our greatest strength lies precisely in our interdependence and that variations in affective fuels, as long as they don't make us discriminate against others, in effect offer variability and adaptability to the environment. We need to understand that the affective fuels and the fear of nonexistence account for discrimination and for violence in our society, and we need to be selective in how we choose to integrate the sense of self against this fear. In essence, we are polarized by the fear of nonexistence when we feel threatened by the loss of an affective fuel of ego integration by other individuals.

In a prior chapter, I said that when dealing with a patient, therapists have three options: reinforcement, substitution, or introspection. Of the three, introspection is the only one that offers the chance to free us from being enslaved by the affective fuels. Understand that the acquisition of affective fuels is not a bad thing per se. After all, it has led to many inventions and advancements that have helped society and made life easier for millions. What we need to do is control the affective fuels that integrate us and realize that we are only inasmuch as we do for others. We need to put a bridle on the horse. We need to control the sense of self and understand that, as a mechanism of evolution, it has limitations. If instead of fighting against one another trying to assert our individuality we were able to realize the sense of union in one another, we would go a long way. We all have a desire to belong that satisfies the desire for union, which results from the sensation of incompleteness that we felt when we separated from the absolute with the taking of consciousness (original sin).

In the process of losing oneself in activities or others, the self disappears, the individual becomes one with the process, and in that state, the realization of union takes place as opposed to the fragmentation of union.

So how do we accomplish this change? We need to start by educating our children about the nature of the self. This might seem a tall order, but failure to do so would result in major social conflicts, pain, and suffering.

- We teach our children about sexual education and driving education, but we do not teach them about the nature of the self and its mechanisms. Courses should be instituted in elementary or high school to start teaching our children the mechanism of ego integration so they can understand why they feel the way they feel.

- Ideologies and religious belief systems that preach discrimination, superiority, or demeaning of individuals who do not share those belief systems have to be regulated because they constitute mechanisms of ego integration that will eventually lead to division, conflict, and warfare.

- Compassion, selflessness, and forgiveness should be the driving force behind all our actions. This has to be taught in all the schools.

- We need to understand that culture is a conglomeration of affective fuels, which include language, customs, architecture, ideology, and so on. All help to integrate the self against nonexistence. Understanding geography in the past accounted for the divergence of language, ideas, and cultures, and now communication is accounting for a convergence of these cultures and ideas and the development of conflicts when different affective fuels come in contact with one another. Understanding that we're not at the point yet where there is a common culture and language, we need to accept that different individuals would prefer to stay with their respective affective fuels. In view of this, immigrants to a country should be required to integrate with the same values and language as a precondition to integration and assimilation. This will avoid social upheaval and social division within each particular culture. Witness what is happening in Europe now, with no-go zones.

- In order to achieve unity, we need to start by having a common language so that people can communicate regardless of their culture. The universal language should be taught in the schools to facilitate this transition.

- A common set of values with respect for individuals' basic human rights (i.e., life, freedom of religion, equality, freedom of speech, freedom of thought, etc.) has to be instituted at a universal level. Theocracies cannot be allowed since they promote one religion over another and by their nature discriminate against opposing religions. Very commonly adherents to one religion will claim discrimination in a country where it did not originate, while in their own country they actively discriminate against minority religions. This is a double standard that should not be tolerated. They need to be called out on it. Remember that religion is one of the strongest affective fuels because it answers directly the fear of nonexistence. We need to understand that no religion can claim superiority over another religion since all religions claim to be the one and only true religion. Understanding that they all answer our profound fear of nonexistence, we must respect each individual's decision to follow one religion or another without discriminating against the individual for this choice. The US Constitution seems to be a good starting point to develop universal values of freedom and basic human rights. It appears to be one of the most advanced instruments of human rights ever written. But human rights based on a religious concept have to be avoided. All religions stake a claim to be the real one, but many of them discriminate against individuals who do not believe like they do. Since we cannot be certain of which one is correct and all claim to be so, the most equitable approach is to adopt human rights based on individual freedoms and not religious tenets. People would then be free to practice their religions on an equal basis with everyone else but without the preference of one over another. Failure to do so will lead to more wars and division.

- Based on the above, as human rights are respected and a common languages develops, a convergence of culture would tend to happen spontaneously. It would take generations for this to take place, but the advancement of communications and social media are accelerating this process. That's why it is so important to have basic human rights to govern this convergence. Compassion must always be the driving force. Another form of convergence that is taking place now is a genetic convergence.

As there is more communication, cultures are brought together in the form of affective fuels, as are individuals. This admixture of different races generates a genetic convergence. So we are changing not only culturally, intellectually, technologically, and religiously but also genetically, and this is leading toward a common culture and language. Individuals may seek out a particular culture (understand a collection of affective fuels) because they were born into it or because they have more affinity with it due to their upbringing. We tend to preserve our sense of culture because we feel safe in it, and we reject or fight against a different culture for the same reason. We have two options: one is to accept this convergence and admixture of cultures, which will result in a new culture by itself that is hopefully more tolerant and humane, and the other option is to preserve the different cultures, understanding that these cultures are mechanisms of self-protection, and become tolerant of the differences among them without feeling threatened in our own. There are pros and cons to each approach. The approach of homogenization has the advantage of increased communication, better understanding, and the ability to see one another as human beings. The disadvantage of homogenization is that if the culture fails to promote humanization, cooperation, and peace in our society, it will be a dead end for our species. In addition, it may dampen social and technological advances by making people pursue certain goals and neglect others that they do not consider valuable. The advantage of the diversification of cultures is that it provides a buffer against evolutionary catastrophes. It may also allow for individuals to move freely among different countries, depending on which culture or set of affective fuels they find more affinity with, in order to integrate themselves. By having different cultures, individuals may pursue different goals because of different affective fuels, which may result in technological, social, and scientific advances. The disadvantage of diversification is that it can lead to conflict as people feel threatened by the different cultures (understand affective fuels). A middle-of-the-road approach would be to preserve the cultures since they enrich our lives with the excitement of seeing new and different affective fuels at work but at the same time understanding the mechanisms of ego integration so that we see the relativity of affective fuels as mechanisms of ego integration and don't fall into the trap of thinking that we are less because we are different and generate conflicts.

- Individuals must be taught that the concept of self is an evolutionary process that is necessary for the evolution of the species. We must also understand that we need to put a bridle on this process so that it is not unchecked, where it could do harm. Both capitalism and communism are based on the concept of acquisition of material affective fuel. Whereas capitalism seeds the mechanism of division, communism seeds the mechanism of oppression. There is no transcendental difference between them since they are both based on the desire for acquisition of material affective fuel, one way or the other. Actual transcendence would involve understanding the need for this desire for acquisition and liberating the individual from this desire (think of Mother Teresa of Calcutta).

- Emphasis should be placed on the interdependence that we will have on one another in society and the need to value and cherish this interdependence. Instead of looking at others as competitors, we should look at them as allies. This would only happen with a profound change in the perception of the concept of the self from something solid and static to something that is pliable and an adaptive mechanism of evolution.

Unless we are able to change and understand the mechanisms of integration at a deeper level, the divisions that we are experiencing, the conflicts, and the wars will increase exponentially to the point that we will be wiped out as a species. We will then become another dead end of evolution.

Let us govern ourselves accordingly.

Printed in the United States
By Bookmasters